# BRISTOL
# CURIOSITIES

Julian Lea-Jones

BIRLINN

First published in 2007 by
Birlinn Ltd
West Newington House
10 Newington Road
Edinburgh EH9 1QS


www.birlinn.co.uk

ISBN 13: 978 1 84158 589 5
ISBN 10: 1 84158 589 0


British Library Cataloguing-in-Publication Data
A catalogue record for this book is available from the British Library


Edited by Katy Charge
Design by Andrew Sutterby


Printed and bound by 1010 Printing International Ltd, China

# CONTENTS

# ACKNOWLEDGEMENTS

To Birlinn Limited for the idea, especially Katy Charge and Susan Sutterby their advice and support. To Diane, my wife, love and appreciation for cheerfully reviewing many drafts, often at unsociable hours and for coping with piles of books and papers scattered around the house, and to my son Christopher for his drawings of the Angel Fountain.

To my friends and members of Temple Local History Group – whose researches and adventures provided the basis for many of these stories.

To Captain Walter Jafee, Frank Markus and Hugh Roberts for information about the Liberty Ships; Marmaduke Alderson, former Lord Mayor of Bristol for pictures of AE1; Marc Vyvyan-Jones for illustrating Bristol's sinister history; Roger Skuse, landlord of the Port of Call in Clifton for the Sailor's Prayer; Martyn Bird for his father, James Edward (Ted) Bird's sketches; Jean Farrugia and Sid Bowen, Post Office Archives; Howard Knight, Chief Information Officer at Lloyd's BIC, for the Lutine Bell information; Dave Wheeler, swanherd at Abbotsbury Swannery, Dorset; John Powell, Ironbridge Gorge Museum Librarian, for the Coalbrookdale fountain data; the late Reginald Gibbs, Langfords' senior clock maker, for bequesting personal notes; Andy Nicholls and Sir George White for horological help; Joyce Williams for her eloquent poem; Nicholas Cox for his drawing of Temple Church tower. To many authors, particularly Eileen Gooder, whose extensive research into the crusading orders helped place Bristol's establishment in the wider perspective; Peter Davey, for his bus timetable; Professor Neil L. York, Brigham Young University for 'The Arsonist as Revolutionary'; Churches Conservation Trust's Rob Hendy, their 'cutlass finder'; Stephen Grey-Harris for Tudor silver values; Anthony Beeson, the Central Library's Fine Art Librarian, for his drawings; Jim Fussell and Dr Howard Falcon-Lang, lecturer in Palaeontology at the University of Bristol, for their expert opinions; John Williams the City Archivist and his staff for information on Messrs Sturge's proposal; Frances Charlton and Christopher Williams for making the Baily project possible and Caroline Jordan for artistic insights into his work.

Although I seem to have spent more time checking the manuscript than in writing it, my worry is that there are still errors – all I can say is mea culpa and hope that they do not spoil your read.

# 1

## BRISTOL: THE 'CRADLE OF AMERICA'

The name 'Bristol' is supposed to mean 'the place of the bridge', but as any cyclist will tell you, it also means 'the city of hills'. Was it these hills, seven like Rome, that gave our ancestors their curiosity bump? The need to know what lay on the other side of the hill would have been driven by more than just idle curiosity, it would also have been a matter of survival. Nowadays the tourist industry advertises Bristol as the 'Gateway to the Southwest', restating a fact that our kingdom's rulers and quite a few entrepreneurs looking for new lands to exploit have recognised for centuries.

To the Saxons, Bric was a border town between Mercia and Wessex, and for the Romans, Abonae (now the suburb of Sea Mills) merely a convenient jumping-off point for subjugating Wales. The town's strategic position at the confluence of two rivers, the Avon and the Frome, and with easy access to the Severn Sea explains why William the Conqueror built his second largest castle here.

Of the many variations of the city's early names Bristowe is probably the most recognisable to modern ears. The general story of how this became the modern name of Bristol, is explained by a local dialect practice of adding an 'L' to words with vowel endings thus changing the pronunciation of Bristowe to Bristol. This local characteristic also resulted in changing the word for the birth of an objective into one meaning a perfect attainment, which, if one wanted to be flippant, could explain how so many explorers became fired up by this linguistic mistake and believed that Bristowe would be an ideal place to achieve their great idea of being the first to find the fabled islands and riches of Brasyle. On a more serious note, it might help to delve into the early records to see how it was that Bristol became a centre for exploration of the New World.

Bristol's strategic location, recognised and exploited by William the Conqueror, would have been based upon knowledge of the fact that this was already a major port and trading centre. The success experienced by Bristolian sailors was due in part to the unusually sturdy construction of their ships, and the reasons for this are explained in the chapter 'Ship Shape and Bristol Fashion'. This sturdiness significantly improved their survivability; but there was also an administrative reason for the success of Bristol explorers.

In 1373 the town's unique location and trading importance was recognised by Edward III who, after petitions from the Bristol Merchant Guilds, agreed to make it a county in its own right, independent of both Somerset and Gloucestershire. This early autonomy, together with its continued development as an international port and Bristolians' innate curiosity, made it an ideal centre for exploration and trade, a gateway to the New World, and a rich source of all forms of marketable curiosities such as the 'smoking weed'. However, that was all in the future. To continue the story, we need to go to 1467 during the mayorality of William Canynge, as it was then that the town council decreed that the trade guilds would be responsible for managing the entire town's foreign trade. This resulted in the Merchant Guild, subsequently known as the Guild of Merchant Adventurers, becoming the main supporter and financier for the discovery and colonisation of North America, a close trading relationship that continues today under its modern name of the Society of Merchant Venturers.

Since the fourteenth century sailors working for William Canynge returning from Iceland (at that time his fleet had a Royal monopoly on the Icelandic trade), recounted tantalising stories of western lands and the fabled island of Brasyle. As a result of the continual stories and accounts, apocryphal or otherwise, Bristol merchants developed a fixation with the riches to be gained and started major programmes of exploration. One of these early testing voyages by the Bristol Merchant John Jay III took place in 1480 when, with a small 80-tun ship he set out to find the legendary islands. Sadly nine weeks of bad weather forced him back to the shelter of Ireland. Undeterred there was a steady stream of other hardy souls willing to try their luck. Probably as a result of news of these early voyages and spying, the local zeal for exploration came to the attention of others on the continent, one of whom was Giovanni Caboto, who at that time was living with his family in Venice.

**First Footing Venetian Style**
In 1494 or '95 the Genoese-born Giovanni Caboto, known to us as John Cabot the domiciled Venetian, arrived in Bristol accompanied by

his wife Mattea, and sons Lewis, Sebastian and Sanctus. They set up home in St Nicholas Street, which is marked today by a commemorative plaque on the street wall of St Nicholas Church. His subsequent relationship with the Bristol Merchants appears to have been a marriage of minds and ideals, both literally and dialectically – they wanted his skill as a mariner and geographer, together with his propensity for risk taking, and he needed their financial support. The critical next stage was Royal Assent because this was needed before they could exploit any discoveries they hoped to make. John Cabot and the Bristol Merchant's appeal to Henry VII was successful and on 5 March 1496 the King granted John Cabot letters patent of discovery to search on his behalf for lands hitherto unknown to Christians, but hopefully with lots of gold. It read in part:

> ...full and free authoritie, leave, and power, to sayle to all partes, countreys, a see as, of the East, of the West, and of the North, under our banners and ensignes, with five ships...and as many mariners or men as they will have in saide ships, upon their own proper costes and charges, to seeke out, discover, and finde, whatsoever iles, countreyes, regions or provinces of the heathen and infidelles, whatsoever they bee, and in what part of the world soever they be, whiche before this time have beene unknowen to all Christians.

They then set about raising the money and equipping a single 50-tun ship, in which they sailed from Bristol in the summer of 1496. For a number of reasons, which can be read in the many books about Cabot's voyages, they were forced to return to Bristol after getting only as far as Iceland. John Cabot decided to try again and got more backers, but again only for a single ship, a caravel named *Matthew* believed to be named after his wife Mattea, and by the following spring was ready for the off. Thus it was that on 2 May 1497 John Cabot, accompanied by his son Sebastian and a crew of eighteen Bristol sailors, set off in their minute 100-tun ship to find a landfall in the New World.

A seaworthy, fully functioning replica of the *Matthew* was launched on 9 September 1995 and when not at sea on cruises can be seen moored alongside another of Bristol's maritime firsts, the SS *Great Britain*. It is a sobering thought to look at this small ship and realise that, as small as it

Statue of John Cabot as Tudor mariner in the portico of Council House.

is, it is still 20 per cent larger than the earlier vessel of John Jay, which makes one realise why Jay's ship was beaten by the weather.

The voyage was relatively quick: on 24 June they made landfall and planted the Royal Standard, naming the place St John's, as it was the saint's day, and claimed the land for Henry VII. Not wishing to make the same mistake that Christopher Columbus did five years before, they spent about a month sailing for at least 300 leagues along the coast to check that they hadn't just discovered another Hispaniola. The Cabots first thought that they had found the fabled route to the Indies and Cathay, which could explain why the indigenous population was given the name 'Indians'. The part of the mainland newly discovered by Cabot was the northeastern part of the North American continent now known as Newfoundland.

After some further coastal exploration Cabot and his crew returned safely, this time to a jubilant reception in Bristol. Cabot went to St Mary Redcliffe, where he gave thanks for his safe return, and presented the church with an unusually large souvenir of the trip. The a giant whale bone, can still be seen in the church alongside a model of his ship. The story of the epic voyage is illustrated in one of the stained-glass windows in the south transept.

## The Naming of America

Upon returning from his first two voyages, one of the first people to meet Cabot would have been the customs officer (as always). However, this particular customs officer was also a rich Bristol merchant, and was likely to have been one of the trip's backers. The Chief Customs Officer, as the King's representative in Bristol, was tasked with formally conveying the King's thanks and gratitude, which was expressed in the practical form of a gift of £10 together with a pension of £20 per annum. As one of the trip's backers he would obviously have been well known to John Cabot and it is believed that he was also a personal friend. This friendship and gratitude to the person who enabled John Cabot to realise his dream made it likely, as was often the case, that the King's new-found-land was named after him. The name of the customs officer was Richard Ameryke or Ap Meryke. This is Bristol's explanation for the naming of the land called 'America', although needless to say there are other contenders for the glory of naming the new continent which, based upon surviving records to date, is a good example of historical convergence.

Another much-researched aspect of Bristol's links with the birth of America is to do with the design of the national flag – the Stars and Stripes. There are three contenders for the founding title whose flags had similar design features that all predated the country's declaration of independence: the East India Company; the Washington family of

John and Sebastian Cabot's commemorative plaque near Quay Head.

Sulgrave Manor in England; Ap Meryke or Ameryke. Of these, the only one that was contemporary with Cabot's first landing is that of Richard Ameryke whose flag comprised six vertical stripes emblazoned with three stars – the jury is still out!

The other generally accepted claimant for the naming of America is of course Christopher Columbus; although he didn't actually make landfall on the mainland, he claimed to have discovered the landmass five years earlier. Another possibility is that although Columbus found the land, he believed it to be Asia, and it was not until the Italian navigator Amerigo Vespucci recognised the landmass as a 'new world' rather than Asia that it was named 'America' – after him.

Whilst not wishing to spoil a good story with facts, there is a further possibility that America was not named by either Columbus or Cabot, but by the geographer, Martin Waldseemuller. The *Catholic Encyclopedia* refers to him by his name Hylacomilus and raises the possibility of a fifth option, based upon the fact that when he published his celebrated work *Cosmographiae Introductio* at Saint-Dié in Lorraine in 1507, he referred to the name America for the New World.

The sad news about John Cabot is that he did not survive to draw his handsome pension. The King was so pleased with the results of his second voyage that he proposed a third and much better equipped voyage for the following year, 1498. The patent was for six ships of up to 200 tuns each, which were to continue the previous year's explorations down the coast until they reached Spanish territory. The King even arranged for the financing of the largest ship and the Bristol Merchants financed another four more modestly sized ships crewed by a total of 300 men. They sailed in May 1498, and one of the ships, a lucky one, was soon damaged in a storm and forced to return to England. The rest of the fleet, including John Cabot, were never heard of again, and although a number of books have been written about possible evidence of their successful landings on the North American mainland, no one knows for sure where they ended up.

**Pathfinders to the New Lands**
However sad the loss of John Cabot and his 1498 fleet was, his discoveries provided the impetus for many more voyages of exploration, some more successful than others, that paved the way for the British settlement of the New World. Although this is not intended to be a treatise on the subject of all the Bristol voyages, a look at some of the key people and the part that they played either as explorers or sponsors will give an idea of the sheer doggedness displayed by our ancestors who risked both their lives and pockets to open up the riches of the new lands across the ocean. I hope that it will also show why Bristol can justifiably claim to be the cradle of America.

John Jay jnr, a merchant and shipowner, took part in a 1480 voyage. Although the voyage itself was unsuccessful, he survived the storms and was able to return to Bristol, becoming Sheriff of the city in 1493. There is a memorial brass to him in the church of St Mary Redcliffe.

The year 1603 saw the beginning of the main thrust of colonisation, with an expedition captained by the 23-year-old Martin Pring. His two ships were the *Speedwell* and the *Discoverer*, which were financed by a prominent Bristol merchant and philanthropist, John Whitson. One of the objectives of the expedition was to search for suitable landfalls and medicinal plants such as sassafras. They landed first in what is now New England on the Maine coast, probably around Penobscot Bay. Continuing their quest, they sailed southwest and arrived in Cape Cod Bay in early June. Martin Pring, quite understandably, named his significant discovery Whitson Bay in honour of his sponsor. This was an astute move as his sponsor, as well as being a prominent merchant, was also, at various times, an Alderman, Sheriff, Mayor and Member of Parliament for Bristol. One of Whitson's legacies was the founding of the Red Maids School in Bristol (now at Westbury-on-Trym), and his tomb is in the crypt of St Nicholas Church in the city. The school holds an annual Founder's Day candlelight service on around 17 November. Martin Pring, who went on to become commander of the naval forces of the Dutch East India Company, also has a memorial in Bristol that can be seen in St Stephen's Church. I have a personal interest in this expedition because it was my tenth great-grandfather, the Reverend Patrick Copeland, who sailed with Martin Pring as chaplain to the fleet. A clue to the reason why the discovery of Whitson Bay was significant lies in its subsequent and more familiar name, that of Plymouth Bay, the place where the Pilgrim Fathers arrived in the *Mayflower* in 1620. The rest, as they say, is history.

In 1610 James VI (James I of England), agreed to grant the Bristol Merchant Adventurers a charter to colonise Newfoundland, which was to become Canada's first official English colony. This planned colonisation was under the leadership of John Guy who became their first Governor. They landed about fifty miles away from St John's, which had been discovered on John Cabot's successful second voyage, at a place named Cuper's Cove (the present-day settlement of Cupids). Their arrival, armed with a royal charter, was complete with a shipload of livestock including heifers, bulls and goats. There were also sixteen women passengers, presumably to help establish the colony. However, the ship's arrival was not well received by the resident fishermen who had established a cod-fishing and salting settlement, after Sebastian Cabot, John's son, had discovered – or rediscovered – the rich fishing grounds. The establishment of a very successful cod-salting industry, known as stock fish, became in itself a key factor in England's ability to feed its sailors on extended voyages and so open up the southern coasts to further colonisation. The cod fishermen understandably saw the official colonists' presence as an intrusion and a threat to their business. However, after three years, the colony known as the Sea Forest Plantation was left to fend for itself as their Governor John Guy decided that his business interests back in Bristol took precedence.

The year 1615 brought better news for the abandoned colony with the arrival of John Barker from Bristol. He bought land there under what was now the King's Charter and established a successful colony. Followed by Bermuda (the group of islands in the North Atlantic), Newfoundland is the United Kingdom's oldest colony.

The year 1631 saw another explorer, Captain Thomas James, set off in search of the fabled Northwest Passage to the Pacific. During his search, on 17 June, he discovered and made landfall on Resolution Island and named the haven 'Harbour of God's Providence' (James Bay). He continued his explorations and during that summer and autumn he went on to discover in July, Nottingham and Digges Islands, followed by Port Nelson and then Charlton in October. Unable to return that year he endured a winter of privation and hardship on the mainland, but as soon as the weather eased in the following May he went on to discover and name Brandon Hill Island before returning to Bristol with all of this invaluable geographical information. His James Bay became the centre of the great Hudson Bay Company, a company that continues today, the signs for which are abbreviated on their storefronts to HBC. A plaque on the Quay Head on 'the Centre' in Bristol (one of many plaques there erected to remind us of the accomplishments of Bristol's explorers) marks his voyages.

As a result of a loan to Charles II by the Bristolian Admiral Sir William Penn (born in St Thomas parish on 28 October 1644, and whose funeral armour and monument are in St Mary Redcliffe Church), the day of 5 January 1681 marks a milestone in the colonisation of North America. The breakthrough came about because the King was unable to repay the loan and Penn's son, William jnr, a Quaker who had a dream of establishing a colony in America under the Quaker tradition of religious toleration and freedom under law, asked for the outstanding loan to be transferred to him. It was on that day, 5 January 1681, that Penn jnr persuaded the King to commute the outstanding loan owed to his father into a grant of land, which he used as the basis for the colonisation of a vast tract of about 40,000 square miles. This land, now known as Pennsylvania, was named at the request of the King as a memorial to the services William's father had performed for him. Armed with this land Penn was able to encourage people to emigrate by offering 100 acres for a mere 40 shillings (£2). Colonists with more funds could also buy £100 shares in 5,000-acre lots. Not surprisingly this started a land rush with as many as 360 passengers arriving on a single vessel.

The plaque in Queen Square honouring Polish patriot Thaddeus Kosciuszko.

These are just a few of the strong links that exist between America and Bristol. The total list numbers into the hundreds of named people, and it is important to realise that the trade in enterprise has been both ways and continues today. Having mentioned the memorials to the early explorers that can be seen in the church of St Mary Redcliffe, it would be remiss not to mention that the chapel dedicated to St John the Baptist on 24 June, the day of John Cabot's landfall, was named as an American chapel where the friends of the church have donated embroidered kneelers depicting the arms of each of the original thirteen states and seven diocese of America. The Welcome Society of Pennsylvania made a gift of service books to the chapel.

Still on the topic of Bristol being the cradle of America, which also applied after its baptism of fire, when cordial relations had been resumed, Queen Square provided Elias Vanderhorst, the diplomatic representative of the fledgling nation, with its first British Consulate. The house and consulate, marked by a plaque, was also the temporary home to a famous Polish and American patriot, Thaddeus Kosciuszko, discussed in more detail in the chapter entitled 'American Independence and The Ties of Trade'.

## 2

## UNFORSEEN CIRCUMSTANCES

Hindsight, as they say, is a wonderful thing and history is littered with events that can be regarded as key 'what if' moments. The following accounts are two such 'what if' moments, or as they are often referred to, 'hinge effects', and we can only conjecture what a different sort of place the world would be today if the first of the events outlined below had followed a different course.

### Setting the Scene

The story starts at Germinston in Glasgow on 3 October 1692. A well-to-do merchant family by the name of Dinwiddie had a son who in due course went to the local university, graduated and joined his father's business in the counting house (the seventeenth-century equivalent to the finance or accounts department of a modern firm). Having learned the ropes in his father's firm he then made a successful career as a merchant in his own right. The son's name was Robert and it is reasonable to assume that it was his upbringing and early training in his father's counting house that instilled in him the eye for attention to detail that was to stand him in good stead in his subsequent career.

It is thought that he had graduated in around 1710 and spent about ten years as a merchant before embarking upon a career change that was to alter the course of history. By the early 1720s Robert Dinwiddie had joined government service as a colonial administrator and in 1724 he was the Royal Collector of Customs in Bermuda. It was reported that, although he was diligent in his duties, he was also an enterprising trader in his own right and rapidly became the most substantial man of business in Bermuda. He thus would have been in a fortunate position. Having been a successful merchant and having come from a prosperous family it is likely that he would have already had substantial capital to finance his trading ventures – as they say, 'money makes money'.

In the meantime, in New Providence in the Bahamas, problems were being encountered. The Governor, Woodes Rogers from Bristol, had

Robert Dinwiddie.

been forced to return to England because of the state of his health. In his absence the Lieutenant-Governor, George Phenney, had been accused of 'plundering the very iron of the fortifications for profit', whilst his wife sold 'rum by the pint and biscuits by the half-ryall'. In spite of these complaints, Woodes Rogers, by then in London, supported the activities of his lieutenant because, as he said, he also sought to advance the affairs of the colony. Nevertheless, the residents of the colony petitioned the Crown for redress by appointing an Assembly. So in 1729 Woodes Rogers returned to the Bahamas and established an Assembly, and also set about strengthening the defences against pirates.

In Bermuda, the governing council decided that until Government House was refitted in the style that suited the newly arriving Governor of the island, Allured Popple, Robert Dinwiddie had the most appropriate house in which to act as host, so Popple stayed with him. By this time Dinwiddie was the wealthiest man in St Georges (then capital town of Bermuda), and had also become a shipowner. An indication of his relative wealth can be seen in the fact that at a time when the colony's public debt stood at £700 he was able to lend £5,000 to Bermuda businesses at no personal inconvenience. Because of his official role he was also alive to all the 'evils of the existing trade with all its collusive tricks', all of which must have made him a formidable business competitor.

**The Chessboard Pieces Start to Move**
Dinwiddie's knowledge of trade and his reputation for probity, in addition to his understanding of the colonists' needs (such as their

desperate need for copper coinage – in the American colony a coin in common use was the Spanish gold double escudo, commonly known by its French name pistole) and his direct representations, together with the recommendations that the Council of Trade heed his advice, led to Horace Walpole offering him a new post. The post was that of Surveyor-General of Customs for the whole of the Southern District of the American Colonies, and included Jamaica and the Bahamas. This promotion meant that after sixteen years in Bermuda Dinwiddie took over from Woodes Rogers' erstwhile Lieutenant-Governor, the problematic George Phenney, but asked for some important concessions. During his time in Bermuda he had married Rebecca, the daughter of prominent Scotsman, Reverend Andrew Auchinleck. Dinwiddie asked that Bermuda be included within his new jurisdiction, that he be allowed to retain his seat on the governing council, and that his family be allowed to remain there, as he said it was in all their interests that he retain his close ties with the island and make occasional visits. The Lords of Trade did not agree and insisted that he move his base of operations to Virginia where, in 1742, he took up a seat on the governing council. By the end of the decade he had returned to London, but on 4 July 1751 at the age of fifty-nine he was returned to Virginia as Lieutenant-Governor and became Governor only six years later.

At that time many colonists were expressing anxieties about the strong possibility of an impending 'bloody war' with the French. Dinwiddie, as diligent and shrewd in his official capacity as he was in pursuing his business interests, had established a land company with extensive grants across the Alleghenies. The problem was that he could see that these tracts lay across France's own line of expansion, which ran from Canada to its Louisiana settlements and by this time, 1756, the French had already encountered British fur trappers at the Ohio. Dinwiddie persuaded the Virginia Assembly to set up a fund of £10,000 for the protection of the colony's frontiers against the advancing French.

## The Stage is Set
Although he had a generally harmonious relationship with the colonists and the governing council, Dinwiddie's staunch upholding and furtherance of the royal prerogative did at times cause problems.

One very serious issue was to do with his attempts to impose quit-rents on the land grants, payable to the Crown. Until then he had always had a reputation for shrewdness. However, his insistence on the payment of this tax to the amount of a pistole, then worth about £1, each time he certified a land patent with his signature, indicated a serious lack of judgment. This became yet another of the events that added to the American colonists' growing list of grievances, which eventually precipitated the War of Independence.

## The Unfortunate Case of the *Pistole* Fee

Dinwiddie's main adversary on the issue of the *Pistole* Fee was the Virginia-born, London-educated, King's Attorney Peyton Randolph, who was also a member of the Virginia House of the Burgesses. Because of Dinwiddie's intractability on the affair, the House sent Randolph to London to plead their case directly with the government. The *Pistole* Fee case became a *cause célèbre* when Virginia instructed the Crown lawyers, Campbell and Murray to represent them. The colonists won, insofar that the Crown agreed to remove the fee on all land transactions of less than 100 acres. Dinwiddie was incensed at the outcome and although he had already removed Randolph from office whilst he was in London, he decided to further 'punish' the successful Randolph upon his return to Virginia.

The House of Assembly had been promised £2,500 as compensation for the cost of their London mission and the Governor deducted this amount from the defence sum set aside for General Braddock's campaign against Fort Duquesne. On that occasion General Braddock's campaign against the French fort failed, so the question has to be asked: was insufficient funding and hence lack of supplies a contributory factor in the failure?

## The Governor's Adjutant has a Mission

As we have already seen, Dinwiddie and the British Government fully understood that in order to realise the goals of British expansion on the American continent, the depredations of the French would have to be contained. However, the perceptive Benjamin Franklin made the point that, although the British might recognise the problem, the colonies were 'as weak as a rope of sand'. Nevertheless, down in Virginia, Dinwiddie saw that a key element of his strategy was the need to protect the colonists and their lands by a force of trained militia rather than the volunteers that up until then they had relied upon. In what was only a small part of the French and Indian War, which was itself part of a wider conflict known as the Seven Years War, Dinwiddie attempted to remedy the Ohio River situation in November 1753 by appointing a young 21-year-old surveyor as Adjutant for the southern district of Virginia. One of the Adjutant's tasks was to recruit forces to relieve the Ohio River forts, which the French were already overrunning. Outnumbered, the young surveyor was forced on the first occasion to capitulate to the French. However, the situation and problems he encountered during that expedition taught him some valuable lessons – lessons that were obviously well learned.

### The Lieutenant-Colonel Makes his Mark

In 1754 the Adjutant, who by then was a Major in the colonial forces, and who under Dinwiddie's instruction had been organising the recruitment of forces for the colony and for the building of a British fort to counter that of the French, was promoted by Dinwiddie to Lieutenant-Colonel and provided with the necessary instructions and Crown passport to take a letter to the Commandant of the French forces. He was to convey to the Commandant a warning that the Ohio lands had already been claimed by the British Crown and any further French-led encroachment would not be allowed. His reports and notes, which can be seen in the collection at Virginia University, stated that:

> I was commissioned and appointed by the Honourable Robert Dinwiddie, Esq; Governor, &c., of Virginia, to visit and deliver a letter to the Commandant of the French forces on the Ohio, and set out on the intended Journey the same day: The next, I arrived at Fredericksburg, and engaged Mr. Jacob Vanbraam, to be my French interpreter; and proceeded with him to Alexandria, where we provided Necessaries. From thence we went to Winchester, and got Baggage, Horses, &c; and from thence we pursued the new Road to Wills-Creek, where we arrived the 14th of November.

The Lieutenant-Colonel got back to Williamsburg, the capital of the Virginia colony, during the following January and submitted his report to Governor Dinwiddie who, pleased with his handling of the matter, had quickly sent it to the local printers and arranged for it to be distributed – much to the soldier's surprise. This must have done a lot for the soldier's credibility, because as history shows his skill in the affair was undoubtedly noted both by the leaders of the Virginia colony and by those further afield.

By 1757 when the immediate threat posed by the French was resolved, Dinwiddie as Governor nevertheless found himself in the invidious position of trying to enforce a blockade against the French on one side of Virginia while allowing trade with them on the other side. Although he enforced a vigorous embargo on behalf of the Virginia colony and some, such as New Hampshire, followed suit (New Hampshire even imposed the death penalty upon anyone caught trading with the enemy), other colonies turned a blind eye and trade continued.

## The Beginning of the End

By the time of the hated Stamp Act of 1765, during which period mobs attacked loyalist businesses and in particular British customs officers, Dinwiddie had been back in England for seven years. In a way it was probably fortunate for him as he wasn't around to see all his lifetime's efforts on behalf of the Crown turn to ashes.

The continued pressures of office and years of trying to reconcile the irreconcilable had damaged his health to such an extent that he had asked Pitt if he could be relieved of his position. This was granted and 1759 he had returned to England with his family, living first in London, then Bath, and finally in Clifton in Bristol.

## Robert Dinwiddie's Protégé – The Man of the Hour

Meanwhile what of his protégé, the young surveyor whom Robert Dinwiddie had entrusted with the raising of the militia and the building of forts? The young Lieutenant-Colonel, now not so young, had learned his lessons well and as a result had become a General. The year 1767 saw the Virginia House of Burgesses summarising the colonists' case, the introductory clause of which was written by the General, the member who referred to 'Our Lordly masters in Great Britain'. This was the same member who on 10 May 1775 was appointed Commander-in-Chief of the Continental Army. The young Adjutant who had been given that all-important start to his military career was, of course, George Washington. If Robert Dinwiddie hadn't chosen

George Washington, or hadn't returned to England and died in Bristol, would someone else with similar capabilities have appeared, or would the British have won the war, with the result that in 2007 America would still be part of the British Empire?

**Robert Dinwiddie's Memorial**
Robert Dinwiddie died in his seventy-eighth year in Clifton, Bristol on 27 July 1770. According to Marguerite Fedden, author of *Bristol Vignettes*, a memorial tablet was set up in Clifton parish church, St Andrews, by his wife Rebecca Auchinleck and his two daughters. The memorial was on the interior wall until the church was destroyed in the blitz of November 1940. It was made of marble above and slate below and read as follows:

In this Church are deposited the Remains of
ROBERT DINWIDDIE, Esq., formerly Governor of *Virginia*.
Who Deceased July 27th 1770 in the 78th years of his Age.
The Annals of that Country will testify
With what Judgement, Activity, and Zeal he exerted himself In the Public Cause
When the whole North American Continent was involved
in a French & Indian War.
His Rectitude of Conduct in his Government
And integrity in other Public Employments
Add a lustre to his Character which was revered while he lived
And will be held in estimation whilst his Name survives.
His more private Virtues and the amiable social qualities he possessed
Were the happiness of his numerous Friends and Relations,
Many of whom shared his Bounty.
All lament his Loss
As his happy Dispositions for domestic Life
Were best known to his affectionate *Wife & Daughters*.
They have Erected this Monument
To the Memory of his Conjugal and Paternal Love
Which They will ever cherish and revere
With that Piety and Tenderness He so greatly merited.
Farwell Blest Shade, no more will Grief oppress
Propitious Angels guide Thee to thy Rest.

Although Robert Dinwiddie's monument is no more, in Bristol there remains a much earlier and more tangible link with George Washington's family. During the English Civil War the Royalist Colonel, Henry Washington, who was a collateral ancestor of George Washington, was responsible for breaking through Bristol's defences at a point near the current Museum and Art Gallery. His exploit became known as 'Washington's Breach' and is commemorated by a bronze plaque near the spot.

## Another 'What If' in Bristol's History

One of the problems caused by the war with America and subsequent cessation of trade was a shortage of tar. The new colonies in North America had been encouraged to produce pine tar and pitch, because large quantities were always needed by the Royal Navy. The lack of tar from America was made worse because the war with them coincided with the Russian invasion of the Scandinavian countries, which had cut Britain off from its other main source.

Because of the shortage of wood tar a substitute was sought, which came in the form of one of the many inventions patented by Archibald Cochrane, 9th Earl of Dundonald (father of the famous Lord Admiral Cochrane). The Earl, born in 1749, was a naval officer and inventor who lived at Culross and who developed retorts for extracting tar from coal. He had a number of patents, including one granted for the covering of ships' hulls with coal tar to prevent rotting timbers. Sadly his pursuit of scientific activities bankrupted him, which possibly explains why the tar from coal patent appeared in an advertisement on 29 April 1780 in *Sarah Farley's Bristol Journal*. It was bought by Bristol Ironmasters Roberts and Daines.

The next step in the story involves a Leicestershire man, William Butler, who worked for Isambard Kingdom Brunel on the building of the Bristol and Exeter Railway. Brunel soon realised that a preservative was needed for the tens of thousands of wooden railway sleepers. To resolve the problem, in 1843 he asked Butler to come to Bristol to manage a new tar-distilling works at Crews Hole, St Annes. The Crews Hole works, financed by Roberts and Daines, utilised the patent to process the crude coal tar from the local gasworks, which was then distilled to produce creosote. Within twenty years Butler owned the business, the start of a family firm that continues to this day.

It was the success of this firm that allowed William's son Thomas to go to the 1904 Paris Motor Show and buy himself a car, which became the first motorcar to be registered in Bristol. It had the regional registration letters AE, and because it was the first, these letters were followed by the numeral 1. This car was eventually given by the Butler family to the Corporation for the use of the Lord Mayor and ever since then the registration plate AE1 has been transferred from car to car and used continually for the mayoral limousine. Thus, if it was not for the shortage of tar during the American War of Independence and if the solution to the problem had put into motion a different chain of events, chances are that Bristol's Lord Mayor's car would not have registration AE1!

An interesting thought in conclusion: motorists in Bristol who feel alarmed by possible road congestion charges may have mixed feelings to learn that a direct result of the success of Brunel's railway was the motorcar being introduced to our roads in 1904.

Bristol's mayoral limousine – the city's oldest legacy registration plate.

# 3

# AMERICAN INDEPENDENCE AND
# THE TIES OF TRADE

Ever since John Cabot made landfall in North America in the fifteenth century the wellbeing and livelihood of Bristol and America have been inextricably linked, both through good times and bad. For many, as well as sharing a common ancestry (think of the thousands of Bristolians and people from the West Country who set off, or were sent, to forge a new life in the new land), commerce has been the glue that has cemented the sometimes stormy relationship. As can still be seen in any walk around modern Bristol, it was trade with America that provided the funding and foundation for many of our city's modern institutions. Next time you have the opportunity, take a look at the endowment inscriptions on our hospital, St Monica's Care Home, the City Museum and Art Gallery and, of course, Bristol University with its landmark Wills Tower at the top of Park Street. The dominant trade between America, particularly Virginia, was tobacco but it was the philanthropy of the leaders of this industry that both founded and supported many of Bristol's institutions. However, trade was not one-way and the problems experienced by Bristol merchants during the American War of Independence included a major disruption to their export trade, as well as the loss of essential supplies of tobacco and cotton.

## A Trade Under Threat
Let us take just one of the trades as an example, the manufacture of clay smoking pipes, and then look at the effect on a single Bristol firm, that of Israel Carey. Their premises were identified by an archeological study by Reginald Jackson and Roger Price as being at the corner of Castle Street and Broad Weir. According to the shipment records in the Port of Bristol Authority's Presentment Books for the two years preceding the outbreak of war in 1776, Israel Carey alone exported 1,448 boxes of pipes to America.

It is thought that the first clay pipes were made in London shortly after the 'weed' arrived in England from Virginia during the 1580s.

Smoking quickly became so popular that the need arose for large quantities of the fragile pipes, and the rapidly expanding numbers of pipe makers taking up the trade resulted in them incorporating themselves as a craft on 5 October 1619. Although London almost certainly initiated the trade, Bristol was the main source of pipes for the Virginia market from about 1660 right through to the end of the colonial era.

## A Business up in Smoke

Although the exact quantity of pipes per box is not known for certain, Jackson and Price, in their study, estimated from other records that a box would have contained more than ten gross, i.e. more than 1,440 pipes. This would have given an annual average export figure of over a million pipes – and that is just for a single firm. Bristol accounts state that Israel Carey stockpiled a quarter of a million clay pipes in the belief that the war would be short-lived and trade would quickly resume, and although this sounds a colossal quantity it could have only represented a fraction of a year's exports. However, there are no records of any further exports to America until 1790.

Relating these astronomical figures to the value of the trade, an advertisement for the period reveals that short stem white clay pipes 'for the American market' were priced at 1s 4d per gross – not much it seems. But when these figures are factored this gives an export value to the firm of £965 per annum for that single market. In the eighteenth century this represents a significant amount of business lost – and remember the records show that the trade was disrupted for eight years. These figures give some idea of the serious effect on trade caused by the war and it would seem that Israel Carey's optimism was misplaced.

Staying with the example of clay smoking pipes, another famous Bristol firm of pipe makers was the Ring family who exported to Philadelphia, New York, Baltimore, Boston and New Orleans. They exported an average of one million pipes per year for seventy-seven years.

From a layman's point of view the pipes of the period fell into three main classifications: plain and undecorated with a smooth bottom to the bowl; those with a small spur or foot at the bottom of the bowl (the foot enabled a 'live' pipe to be rested upright); and decorated, either a simple incised decoration or moulded – some were even more

An example of a fancy clay smoking pipe exported to America.

elaborately moulded to represent a man's head, making the pipes look superficially similar to the expensive and elaborately carved meer-schaum pipes.

According to the American archaeologist, Ivor Nöel Hume, about 30 per cent of the Bristol pipes found at sites in Virginia have smooth bowls. This style was initially intended for the Native Indian trade, because they more closely resembled Indian pipes. But Hume concluded from the numbers found at Jamestown that the shape was also acceptable to the colonists. Indeed, in the Historical Society of Pennsylvania collection there is a painting of the Indian Chief Tishcohan, showing him proudly wearing a small bag strung from his neck from which protrudes a short stem white clay pipe, possibly from Bristol.

### The War: The Key Events
In April 1775 the first shots of the American War of Independence were fired in Lexington and Concord and by June of that year George Washington had been appointed Commander-in-Chief of the Continental Army. Meanwhile, back in England, August 1775 saw the royal proclamation declare that the King's American subjects were 'engaged in open and avowed rebellion'. This declaration was followed in

Parliament by the American Prohibitory Act, which made all American vessels and cargoes forfeit to the Crown. The date that we all know, 4 July 1776, was the day the colonists signed their Declaration of Independence. This declaration marked the start of a war that many, including Israel Carey, thought would be short – but it dragged on for six bloody years. It was November 1782 before preliminary Articles of Peace were agreed and signed in Paris, with the end of the war being formally proclaimed in February 1783. In September 1792 a consulate was established in a house at what is now 37 Queen Square in Bristol, with Elias Vanderhorst as the first Consul for the new nation of the United States of America.

Any mention of the following names, 'Wills' and 'Virginia', will prompt most Bristolians to automatically supply the associative word – tobacco. A visit to the works of W.D. & H.O. Wills was reported on as part of a series of 'Bristol at Work' sketches in the *Bristol Times* and *Bristol Mirror* during 1883. During one of these visits, a very interesting letter was shown to the reporter, which referred to a cargo of the 'famous weed' that formed the basis of one of Bristol's major industries. The significance of the letter is highlighted by the name of the author (Robert Dinwiddie's protégé), rather than for the prosaic nature of it is content, worded as follows:

Virginia, 25th November 1759,
Gentlemen, Sometime this week I expect to get on board the *Cary* for your house fifty hogsheads of tobacco of my own and Jno. Park Curtis's, which please to insure in the usual manner. I shall also by the same ship send you ten or twelve hogsheads more if I can get them on board in time; but this I believe, will be impractible if Captain Tulman uses that dispatch in loading which he now has in his power to do.

*I am, Gentlemen, Your most obedient humble servant*
*G. Washington.*
*PS. My goods per Captain Yates are arrived in James River, and I thank you for your diligence in sending them. Robert Cary Esq. and Company.*

## Historic Irony or Ironic History?
The chapter entitled 'Unforeseen Circumstances' outlines the possible consequences of Robert Dinwiddie giving the young George Washington the opportunity to develop his military skills. This letter

reminds us that George and his brother were both plantation owners, and would have dealt with the tobacco houses in Bristol as a matter of course. George would have been aware that Bristol was not far from his family's ancestral home of Sulgrave Manor near Banbury in Oxfordshire and he was probably also aware of the military activities of another of his collateral ancestors, the Royalist Colonel Henry Washington. It was in July 1643, during the English Civil War, that Henry Washington, as part of Prince Rupert's army, broke through the Parliamentary defences during the siege of Bristol.

The besieging of Bristol by Henry Washington on behalf of the King is supremely ironic when we remember that it was just over 130 years later (on 10 May 1775) that George Washington stood up in the Virginian House of Burgesses to declaim *against* their British 'Lords and Masters'. Furthermore, Robert Dinwiddie, who gave General George Washington a start to his military career, was buried in the same church, St Andrew's in Clifton, that Colonel Henry Washington had used as a base from which to attack the Parliamentary forces some 132 years earlier.

## Winners and Losers
Sadly this event serves to remind us that there has never been a war that didn't divide families intellectually, even if they were not actually fighting on opposite sides during the same conflict. When the War of Independence commenced, and trade between England and America came to an effective standstill, the colonial planters had to find new markets for their tobacco. The European traders, particularly the Dutch, who had for a long time been recognised as tobacco experts, already had a large tobacco auction market in Amsterdam, and as major competitors in the trade, were only too happy to capitalise on the conflict and build up their business at Britain's expense. At the outbreak of the war, in Bristol alone there were nearly twenty tobacco merchants engaged in the trade with America, many of whom faced financial ruin. Even at the beginning of that century when Bristol's shipping amounted to only 6,000 tons, Bristol MP Sir John Knight, in response to a Parliamentary question, said that half of Bristol's shipping was accounted for by tobacco imports. With a hogshead, or 'tierce' as they were known, of tobacco weighing about 900 pounds, this would have amounted to about 8,000 hogsheads. To give an idea of the amount of trade disruption caused by the war, a single tobacco

bond, such as that now home to the Create Centre and the City Archives (the Bristol Record Office) in B Bond in Smeaton Road, would have held nearly ten times this amount. The 'tobacco bonds' – still a familiar term in Bristol, although some have been demolished in recent years – still dominate the skyline of south Bristol. Their name derives from a place where goods are stored under the control of customs and excise and tobacco bonds are the places where tobacco entering the country, if stored in a secure locked 'Bond' under customs control, is not subject to excise tax until removed. The tax on what could be anything up to 28,000 tons represents a lot of cash. Sometimes the tobacco would be kept in bond for up to two, or even three years, so the tobacco in Bond represented a significant easing of the company's cash flow.

## Champions and Fence Sitters

At the outset of the war, although those with business and personal dealings sympathised with the colonists, there were those who thought that the most expedient solution was to be seen to support the King, and 'give the colonials a good trouncing and bring them to heel'. On the other side of the fence were those such as Edmund Burke and Henry Cruger, Members of Parliament for Bristol, who foresaw the damage to Bristol's trade and because of this were influential voices for moderation, unfortunately to no avail. Cruger was one of those adversely affected by the war and who certainly had a vested interest in trying to keep the local situation as calm as possible. He also exemplified the point made in the opening paragraph of this chapter about the strong bonds between Bristol and America. Because of his unique career and the key role he played in Bristol's politics during those troubled times, it is worth looking at his career in more detail.

In 1757 a live-wire eighteen-year-old New Yorker arrived in Bristol. His name was Henry Cruger and he lived at No. 1 Great George Street, the house on the corner with Park Street, now marked by a plaque. Having married locally, Henry, who traded as 'Cruger and Mallard' from No. 99 The Key (Quay), prospered in Bristol and became a leading merchant with his attainments reading like a roll call of the city's offices. At that time civic office was only open to Bristolians, either born or connected through a local marriage (interestingly another 'outsider' who brought wealth and fame to the city

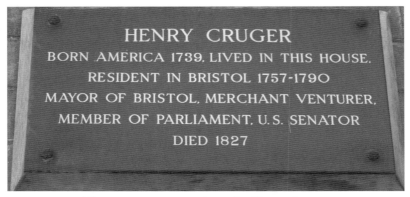

The commemorative plaque for Henry Cruger.

was Woodes Rogers who had also married locally). During Henry's many years in Bristol he held the various offices of Councillor, Sheriff, Mayor, Member of Parliament (1774–80), and he was also elected Master of the Society of Merchant Venturers. He was elected MP again from 1784 to 1790 after which point he returned to his homeland, not to retire but to become a Senator in his home state of New York. However, because of the rules of the Common Council he remained a Bristol Councillor until his death, and therefore was unique in having a representative seat in both America and Britain at the same time. An aspect of the 1831 riots, connected in part with the constitution of the Common Council as a self-elected body, is described in the chapter 'Trials and Tribulations'.

While people such as Edmund Burke and Henry Cruger were trying to calm the situation both locally and through their representations to Lord North's ministry in Parliament, the Bristol Common Council were busy proposing a congratulatory address to George III on the success of his arms in America in the hope that 'seeds of rebellion would be speedily eradicated'. The Council vote was evenly split, but the motion was carried by twenty-two votes because there were twenty absences and two 'lily livered' Whigs decided to support North's ministerialists.

Having decided to support the course of war against the colonials, it was realised that the Royal Navy would need more sailors – leading to a rise in the use of press gangs. The City Council did its bit for the government by offering a bounty to any sailors joining the Royal

Navy, paying out £572 in total during the year. Later that year the Council voted to give the freedom of the city to the Earls of Suffolk and Sandwich, both of whom had been outspoken against the American colonists. The vote had almost certainly been swayed by the news that Britain had lost the Newfoundland fishing trade to the Americans and British ships were even being taken by American privateers in the English Channel. While the Common Council was spending money on recruitment bounties, the Corporation pot of money was shrinking as a direct consequence of the war, and the decline in shipping caused a catastrophic reduction in port dues.

### Sympathy Quickly Turns to Anger When Pockets are Affected

In spite of, or possibly because of this, at a pro-ministerial meeting held in the Guildhall, £21,000 was raised in local pledges in support of the government. Contrast this with the efforts of the preceding week when the Bristol brass merchant J. Scandrett Harford had started a fund for distressed American prisoners of war, which only raised £363. Edmund Burke had also written to a Bristol merchant, saying that local [council] support for Lord North's government 'made America abhor the name of Bristol'.

Another commercial victim of the war was Thomas Farr, who was forced to sell his Blaise Castle estate. He sold it to Mr Skeate, who after only a few years sold it to Harford, who still had sufficient funds to develop the estate and employ Beau Nash to lay out Blaise Hamlet to the latest fashionable 'romantic rustic' design. In 2007 Nash's rustic cottages at Blaise are still occupied as private homes.

By about August 1779 the Anti-American Committee in Bristol had raised 1,306 men for service and established a new subscription fund in order to raise a further 1,000 infantry for service in America.

During this unsettled period one of the many events associated with the prevailing sentiments was the case of Jonathan Britain who was convicted of forgery and hung at the Bewells Cross Gallows at the top of St Michael's Hill. He had been a contributor to the anti-ministerialist paper, 'The Whisperer' and in an attempt to get off the forgery charges he claimed to be involved with the pro-American arsonist responsible for both the Portsmouth Dockyard fires and those at Bristol. This was a seriously bad move on his part as the arsonist was caught and hung for treason (read more about the arsonist Peter the Painter in the chapter

'Bizarre Beliefs and Odd Occurrences'). As a supposed informer, Britain hoped to be able to claim the royal pardon that had been announced in the *Royal Gazette*, but his confession was proved to be a falsification and he was hung.

At this time the White Lion Inn and the adjacent American Coffee House in Broad Street (the site now occupied by the Grand Hotel), was a favourite haunt of Bristolians who were in agreement with King George's policy towards America. Consequently, in spite of the entreaties for reason from Edmund Burke and Henry Cruger, it was the venue for frequent anti-American demonstrations and speeches. Probably the most notable of these disturbances was the tarring and feathering of effigies of Samuel Adams and John Hancock. They were targeted by the mob because they were both known to have been signatories of the American Declaration of Independence of 4 July 1776. The effigies were then hung outside the American Coffee House.

It is interesting to note that John Hancock's name would have been well known to the King's sympathisers in Bristol because he had been instrumental in nurturing the American revolution. Born in 1737 in Massachusetts, and a Harvard graduate, he came to London to represent his wealthy uncle's business interests. When his uncle died in 1763 Hancock inherited what was said to be the greatest body of wealth in New England, which put him in amongst the mainly loyalist society. In spite of his wealth and social Royalist contacts he became increasingly involved with revolutionary politics and supported the move for independence from Great Britain. In this he was at one with the leaders of the New England republican movement and those such as the Adamses. Hancock was elected to the Boston Assembly in 1766, and was also a member of the Stamp Act Congress. In 1768 his sloop *Liberty* was impounded by British Customs in the harbour at Boston on a charge of running contraband goods. As a result, a group of Boston citizens who supported Hancock attacked the customs post and the officers and burned the customs launch. The action of the customs officers might have been the final straw that confirmed Hancock's allegiances; soon after this he supported the Boston Tea Party and subsequently put his name to the Declaration of Independence.

In 1778 there were increasing difficulties in recruiting troops and sailors to fight in America and in the following year an Act was passed by Parliament to conscript anyone able bodied and not in a lawful industry to service in the army for five years. However, volunteers were given a bounty of 3 guineas (£3 3s ), to which the Bristol Corporation added a further guinea.

Shortly before the end of the war both Burke and Cruger stood for re-election. However, many of Burke's supporters had been ruined by the war with America through the disruption to their trade, which partly explained why their re-election failed. Another reason why Burke's re-election failed was because his changed views alienated many of his supporters. I wonder how many of those selfsame disgruntled merchants had been among the Broad Street crowd when the effigies of Adams and Hancock were hung outside the American Coffee House? The following year, because of the death of an MP, the seat became vacant and Cruger, as an American, stood for 'reconciliation and resumption of trade'. Standing against him (with George III's approval) was George Daubeny, for the anti-American ministerial party. The campaign was a nasty one. Reports of the day quoted a dinner at the Full Moon Hotel in Stokes Croft, put on by Daubeny for all his campaign supporters, at which they were asked to taste the difference between Roast Beef of England and American Bull Beef. A toast was proposed to 'Friend of King and Constitution'. When Cruger was told of this, he was heard to say that without him 'they would have had neither beef nor ale'.

## Protest Tragically Curtailed

Daubeny won the Bristol seat by nearly a thousand votes and during the subsequent demonstrations of support and celebrations a party of Cruger supporters took offence at the signal flags and pennons flying on a ship at the quayside. The party shouted at the sailors on the ship ordering them to lower the flags, which was met with abuse from the sailors. Cruger's supporters responded by throwing rocks and other missiles at the sailors. At this point three of the sailors who were either scared or drunk decided to take drastic action to defend themselves by turning one of the ship's guns onto the dockside protestors. Two were killed outright with many more injured. It says much for the prevailing political climate that the subsequent court verdict was one of 'justifiable homicide'. Until the bombing of Bristol during the Second World War, a memorial to those killed was in Temple Church yard. The inscription was unusual, indeed probably unique, in that the text in their memory read: 'Inhumanely murdered by three men whose names appear here'.

## The Turning Tide

When the Prime Minister, Lord North, resigned on 22 March 1782 forever after marked as 'the man who lost us the colonies', the name 'American Coffee House' next to the White Lion became an embarrassment to its customers and it was changed to British Coffee House. Bristolians had to wait for over two centuries for the return of American coffee houses to the city.

## From Guns to Mustard

Down the centuries Bristol has provided a safe haven for refugees from other lands, many of whom have enriched our city and country. The list is too long to enumerate here, yet there is one who was recognised as a patriot, both in his native Poland and in his adoptive home, America, and who also has a memorial in the centre of Bristol. His name was Thaddeus Kosciuszko. I mention him here because he was another of those remembered in Bristol who was also involved in the American War of Independence, although he didn't visit Bristol until 1797, after it was over. Kosciuszko had been one of those supporting the struggle of the Poles against the Russians, and as a young army captain had received his military training in France before going to America to gain practical experience. He rose to the rank of Brigadier General in George Washington's army, being the principal designer of the Delaware River forts, as well as defences at Saratoga and West Point during the War of Independence. After the war he went on to become 'Architect of the Capitol' and for this and for his role as an American Independence Patriot he is honoured by a memorial bust in the Capitol in Washington DC. There is also a plaque to his memory in Queen Square, Bristol, where he stayed at the home of Elias Vanderhorst. However, a more prosaic memorial to him can be found daily across the United States – his name has been given to a brand of mustard, packaged in sachets and usually found in burger bars! Enquiries reveal that this is not as banal as it sounds – Kosciuszko Mustard is an ingredient of many traditional Polish recipes.

# 4

## A MARINER'S TALE

When you stand in front of the pink-washed walls of the Mariners' Almshouse at the end of King Street, close to Marsh Street, apart from the cries of seagulls and the signboard on the front of the almshouse there is little indication of its nautical connections. The large elaborately lettered board, itself a reminder of a bygone age, proclaims that the residents are:

> Freed from all storms the tempest and the rage
> Of billows, here we spend our age.
> Our weather beaten vessels here repair
> And from the Merchants' kind and generous care
> Find harbour here; no more we put to sea
> Until we launch into Eternity.
> And lest our Widows whom we leave behind
> Should want relief, they too a shelter find.
> Thus all our anxious cares and sorrows cease
> Whilst our kind Guardians turn our toils to ease.
> May they be with an endless Sabbath blest
> Who have afforded unto this rest.

Before passing by, read it and give a thought to the seamen who, having spent a life braving the dangers of the oceans of the world, at last came to this haven from both storm and bullying bosun. Although calls of the watch are now replaced by the noises of traffic, and the bosun's pipe by police and ambulance sirens, there are still stories to be told.

The almshouses formed three sides of a quadrangle, but what you see before you today are the repaired and restored remains. The East Wing and the Merchants' Hall were destroyed in the blitz of the Second World War and replaced by an office block. The only clue to the office block's past history and the fact that many centuries ago it was the site of a chapel dedicated to St Clement is a small bronze plaque on the front wall. St Clement was the first of the apostolic fathers, who on the orders of the

Commemorative plaque on the site of St Clements Chapel.

Roman Emperor Trajan, was drowned by being tied to an anchor and thrown into the sea. His saint's day is 23 November, and because of his watery martyrdom, he was adopted by mariners as their patron saint. In 1445 the Bristol Gild [Guild] of Mariners erected a chapel on this spot dedicated to St Clement and St George and provided a chantry priest to pray for the souls of departed mariners. As well as their spiritual salvation, the Gild also provided earthly help by establishing an almshouse for twelve poor mariners but when Henry VIII called for the dissolution of the chapels and chantries, the Gild ceased to function. However, the mariners' wellbeing was taken into consideration when in 1552 Edward VI agreed to grant a royal charter to the Master, Wardens and Commonality of Merchant Venturers of the City of Bristol. This enabled the Merchant Adventurers or Venturers (the title was used interchangeably) to use the site of the former chapel to build a hall, and to reinstate an almshouse for twelve poor mariners. Apart from the initial financial support from the society, day-to-day funding came from a levy of a penny ha'penny on every ton of the merchant's goods shipped through the port and each Bristol sailor contributed a penny in the pound from their wages. These levies were also intended to fund a free school for the sailors' children and to provide a new chapel, more conveniently located at Shirehampton, to be nearer the ships' Hungroad moorings.

No doubt through the centuries these plain pink walls have heard many an amazing story from ancient mariners. One such character is worthy of further discussion here as he is possibly the most famous, but incorrectly named, resident.

The Mariners' Almshouse in King Street.

## The Story as Generally Told

The story starts with an encounter on a Bristol street in the last quarter of the eighteenth century. In all probability it was on one of the dockside streets that Lady Luck finally smiled on the elderly seaman when she directed his footsteps to a local merchant. The old man, obviously penniless and in ill health, asked the gentleman if he might use his influence to get him an admission pass to the workhouse, then St Peter's Hospital in the city. He explained that he had no family left; he had outlived two wives, and both his sons had been killed, and because of this he was just asking for a final shelter where he too could die in peace. The accounts explain how the merchant found a place for him in the Mariners' Almshouse.

A number of Bristol histories tell the story of this mariner, 'Llewelyn Penrose', supposedly just another retired seaman, living out his last years in the haven provided by the Merchant Venturers. The various accounts all explain that Penrose, who had gone to sea from Bristol as a young lad, had been shipwrecked and the journal of his adventures contained tales of pirate treasure, complete with maps and cryptic clues. The accounts also tell how the young Edgar Allan Poe, visiting Bristol, was introduced to the ancient mariner and was so inspired by his tale that he used it as the basis for one of his most famous stories, *The Gold Bug*.

**Truth – Stranger Than Fiction**

The truth behind the oft-repeated story is more fascinating and even more curious than the fiction. However, the greatest and saddest revelation came after the death of the ancient mariner, whose name turned out to be not Llewelyn Penrose, but William Williams. He had another claim to fame that had nothing to do with the sea. Yes, he had been a mariner, but years before he had fallen on hard times. He had taught the Royal Academy's second President, and had been responsible for putting his feet on the first rungs of the ladder to artistic fame and glory.

William Williams was a Bristolian of Welsh descent who was born and lived in St Augustine's parish. He was baptised on 14 June 1727 in the church of St Augustine the Less, College Green (damaged in the Second World War and the remains were demolished to make way for the Royal Hotel extension). He lived within sight of the quaysides where often there were so many ships moored up unloading and taking on cargo that it was said that the sight of all the ships' masts made the quayside look like a forest. William was educated at a local grammar school, but did not take to book learning; it seems that his head was turned by the sailors' yarns of adventures and the sights to be seen in far-off lands, and he was fascinated by the sights and sounds of ships. Like many a lad he ran away and got a berth on a ship. He took to a life at sea and sailed twice to Virginia, before the fates intervened in a way that would have far-reaching consequences.

Sea of masts along The Grove.

34

On a voyage in 1745 his ship was wrecked on the Moskito coast of South America (at that time it was a Spanish colony that was ceded to Britain by the local paramount chief, until it became part of Nicaragua in 1894). Williams spent two years there living among the Rama Indians until in 1747 he was able to get a passage on a ship to America. During his time with the Indians he had taken up painting, and after arriving in America he decided that perhaps the life of a sailor wasn't for him and decided to stay in Philadelphia, where he earned his living as an artist and by teaching. His paintings can still be seen in collections around the world. Paintings such as the portrait of Deborah Hall, dated 1766, can be seen in the Brooklyn Museum's Luce Centre for American Art. Another example, *Portrait of a Boy*, painted in the early 1770s is in the Metropolitan Museum of Art, New York collection. Although portraits weren't his only subjects, within America's emerging post-colonial society, portraiture probably paid the best.

During his enforced stay in South America he had kept a journal of his adventures and some of these he recounted to one of his early art pupils, the young son of a Quaker family from Springfield (now part of Swathmore, just outside Philadelphia) in Pennsylvania. The name of that pupil was Benjamin West. The relationship between Williams and West is important because it influenced later events in both their lives. Precocious and talented, Benjamin was painting portraits from the age of eight, and in later years he became a significant influence on other American painters. In 1760 he went to Italy, where he worked for three years before moving to London in 1763. Upon arrival his style soon came to royal attention, and he became 'Historical Painter to King George III'. As one of the founders of the Royal Academy with Joshua Reynolds he succeeded him to the presidency. At the height of his fame, in his biography he claimed to be self taught. However, in later years, when a manuscript copy of William Williams' journal was shown to him, he agreed that, 'Had it not been for him [William Williams], I should never have been a painter.'

## Llewelyn Penrose

In addition to his painting, William Williams wrote up his own journal, but in the form of the adventures of a fictional Bristol seaman, Llewelyn Penrose. His journal contained all the classical elements of a ripping yarn, with tales of pirate treasure and cryptic clues that a reader would need in order to find the treasure. Llewelyn also started a book called *Lives of Painters*. During his time in America he married twice, and had at least two sons. At some stage he moved from Philadelphia to New York and in 1759 is reported to have had a third son, William Joseph Williams, who followed in his footsteps and became a painter. His best-known portraits are those of Presidents Washington, Adams, and Jefferson. Williams survived both of his wives and on the night of 16 June 1775, he suffered further tragedy when two of his sons were killed at what was generally known as the Battle of Bunker Hill (more correctly the Battle of Breed's Hill, which was across the valley, at Charlestown in Massachusetts) in the American struggle for independence.

**Homecoming**
Understandably depressed by these family tragedies and suffering from homesickness, he was befriended by a gentleman also returning to England, who invited him to accept a sinecure position as 'painter in residence' on his country estate. He accepted but when his patron died he moved to London and approached his former art pupil, Benjamin West. But some time in the early 1780s he decided to return home to his native Bristol, where he set up shop as an artist at 29 Clare Street. It seemed that the business venture failed and, no longer having a family to whom he could turn in Bristol and in failing health, he approached merchant Thomas Eagles to ask if he could get him a bed in St Peter's Hospital, the workhouse on Peter Street, Castle (currently Castle Park). Eagles immediately realised from his speech and demeanour that the person asking for help was no common vagrant and invited him to his family's house for a meal so that he could learn more about the petitioner's background. Following that first meeting, Eagles' interest and pity was sufficiently aroused for him to make further enquiries into the poor mariner's past. What he learned made him realise that the elderly seaman qualified, not for the workhouse, but as a pensioner in the Mariners' Almshouse, and he made the necessary arrangements. The result of this act of charity was that the seaman's health improved to the extent that he was able to live in relative comfort for many more years than he had hoped for before that lucky encounter. However, another result of this act of charity was to have far reaching literary effects.

Freed from all storms the tempest and the rage
Of billows, here we spend our age.
Our weather beaten vessels here repair
And from the Merchants' kind and generous care
Find harbour here; no more we put to sea
Until we launch into Eternity.
And lest our Widows whom we leave behind
Should want relief, they too a shelter find.
Thus all our anxious cares and sorrows cease
Whilst our kind Guardians turn our toils to ease.
May they be with an endless Sabbath blest
Who have afforded unto us this rest.

Signboard on the Mariners' Almshouse.

Williams and Eagles kept in touch and although there were certain aspects of his past life that Williams was reluctant to discuss, Eagles developed a respect for the elderly mariner and artist. Williams would visit the family and entertain them with tales from his past, and one day he gave Eagles a manuscript copy of his 'Journal of Llewelyn Penrose Seaman'. All of Eagles' family was fascinated by Williams' tales, especially his young son John who, being artistically inclined, took particular interest in Williams' artistic accomplishments.

## The Bequest
There the story would probably have ended if it hadn't been for a bequest. On 27 April 1791, Williams died, and in his will he remembered his friend Thomas Eagles who had listened to him when he was down on his luck, and whose act of faith had given him a new lease of life. Eagles was amazed to discover amongst the effects bequeathed to him were portraits of Williams' wives, a self portrait, an unfinished painting on the theme of Penrose, and his book *Lives of Painters* (which listed 187 of his own paintings that had been produced over a thirty-year period, together with a list of fifty-four painted before

he went to America). The bequest also included his collection of books and his artist's equipment.

## The Story Unfolds

When Thomas Eagles' family gathered around to look at Williams' bequest, his son John suddenly remembered the journal that had been given to them some years before. They found it and sat around to read it, realising that at the time they hadn't fully appreciated it. They found the journal fascinating – so much so that it was reported that young John, who was supposed to be returning to boarding-school, 'missed' his coach in order to finish reading Llewelyn Penrose's adventures.

John did eventually return to school at Winchester College, and went from there to Oxford, qualified, and was subsequently ordained a minister in the Church of England. He had livings in a number of parishes but came back to Bristol as curate of St Nicholas Church, next to Bristol Bridge. As well as his church duties, he also built up a reputation in literary and artistic circles, contributing to a number of publications, including *Felix Farley's Bristol Journal* and *Blackwood's Magazine*. One of his contemporaries was the President of the Royal Academy, Benjamin West, and when Reverend John Eagles showed him a copy of the journal, it gave West a sense of déjà vu – back to the days under Williams' tutelage in Philadelphia some fifty years before. He also recognised certain passages that applied to him, and finally admitted that he owed his start to Williams and also that he hadn't served Williams very well when he had asked for patronage in London in the 1770s. Eagles welcomed the opportunity to learn more about Williams' early time in North and South America as he was planning to write an account of his life. He was hoping that West would be able to fill in the gaps that Williams had been reluctant to disclose those many years before when a guest in his parents' house.

## *The Gold Bug*

*The Gold Bug*, published in 1843, was the title of one of Edgar Allan Poe's most famous stories, which was definitely based upon the tales in William Williams' 'Journal of Llewelyn Penrose Seaman'. But how did the contents of the journal come to Poe's attention? A brief background on the writer and poet's life will help put the elements of the story that started this whole literary adventure into context.

He was born Edgar Poe in 1809 in Boston, Massachusetts (eighteen years after William Williams died), was orphaned, then adopted by a John Allan who had a tobacco trading company in Richmond, Virginia. When trade between England and America resumed after the War of 1812, which lasted until 1815, Allan decided to come to England to open a London office. However, before opening the office and getting six-year-old Edgar (now Allan Poe), into a school, he decided to take a tour of England and Scotland with his family. It is more than likely that he would have combined business with pleasure and used the opportunity to visit Bristol's Virginia tobacco merchants. Edgar attended a Dame school in Chelsea, and a private school in Stoke Newington, before returning to America in 1820.

The most likely link between Edgar Allan Poe and the story of Llewelyn Penrose would have been Reverend John Eagles, who had been familiar with the story ever since he was a young boy and had a connection with Poe through William Blackwood's literary magazine. The other person with detailed knowledge of the journal's contents was Benjamin West, who was also known to the Allans and was in London during the same period. Coincidentally, West died the same year that the 21-year-old Edgar returned to America with his parents, a return caused by the collapse of the tobacco market.

Edgar Allan Poe used many elements of the plots that were in Llewelyn Penrose's journal, in particular the use of the skull to locate the pirate treasure. However, he relocated the setting to an island in South Carolina.

One wonders what William Williams would have thought about the literary hare he unwittingly started when he sat in that steamy South American jungle painting and setting down his ideas for the adventures of his alter ego Llewelyn Penrose.

# 5

## THEY MAY BE PIRATES,
## BUT THEY'RE OUR PIRATES

Bristol has a long maritime tradition some aspects of which, like the River Avon, are murkier than others. The city may not be able to claim to have produced the most pirate captains; but Bristol's were certainly among the most notorious. Also, it is more than likely that most of the pirate ships numbered Bristolians amongst their crews. To find out how this came about and why some were honoured, even knighted, for their nefarious exploits, while others were beheaded, we need to delve into the history books and official records. We also need to learn about the differences between pirates and privateers.

### Pirates
The name 'pirate' is associated with violence, ferocity, cruelty and a merciless treatment of victims, and for the amassing of vast treasures traditionally buried on a desert island. But was this image, supported by ripping yarns such as Robert Louis Stevenson's book 'Sea Cook', published as *Treasure Island*, always true? For some pirates, such as Bristol's own Edward Teach (or Thatch), better known as the infamous Blackbeard, certainly the violence and cruelty is largely true. Sticking lighted matches in your beard, and shooting your first mate just for fun is always guaranteed to impress! Edward Teach served his piratical apprenticeship under the command of another pirate, Benjamin Hornigold. However, Hornigold turned out to be too 'mild' for Teach's tastes and he soon set up on his own. Many pirates such as Blackbeard promoted their fearsome reputation in order to subdue their prey by fear of what they might do, as much as by what they actually did. Robert Louis Stevenson even used him in *Treasure Island* as a role model for awfulness:

> 'Heard of him!' cried the squire. 'Heard of him, you say! He was the blood thirstiest buccaneer that sailed. Blackbeard was a child to

[Captain] Flint. The Spaniards were so prodigiously afraid of him that, I tell you, sir, I was sometimes proud he was an Englishman.'

Robert Louis Stevenson could justifiably have been more specific and used the word Bristolian, as it seems that most of the pirate ships had one or more Bristolians among the crew. Captain Henry Morgan, probably the most successful Bristolian pirate, was knighted for his piratical exploits, and the high spot of his career was probably when he was made Lieutenant Governor of Jamaica. Born in South Wales in about 1634, his connection with Bristol goes back to when, as a boy, he was kidnapped from here, put on a ship to Barbados, and sold to a plantation owner. But for a lucky accident of fate, there he probably would have remained until he died. As it turned out, Oliver Cromwell decided that Hispaniola should be taken from the Spanish and in preparation for the invasion the English fleet called in at Barbados to recruit more crew. This gave nineteen-year-old Henry his chance for freedom; he ran away from his master and joined the fleet.

However, the invasion fleet did not succeed against the Spanish and rather than incur the wrath of Cromwell, they sailed on to capture the easier Spanish possession of Jamaica. Later on, the steady acquisition of Caribbean islands left Charles II with a problem. Because the Royal Navy had insufficient ships to hold on to Jamaica and England's other possessions in the region, Letters of Marque were issued to privateers operating out of Port Royal in Jamaica. From his privateering start, Henry went on to become a privateer captain and then a fleet commander. Although much of his Caribbean activities were piratical, he always made sure that King Charles received a cut of the prize monies, which caused the King to develop a certain deafness in the face of Spanish and French complaints. However, Morgan's big career breakthrough came in 1670 when he commanded a fleet of nearly forty privateering ships. His objective was to capture the Spanish treasure capital of the New World – Panama, but by the time his privateers arrived, the Spanish had been warned about the invasion and had managed to move most of their treasure. This, however, didn't stop Morgan sacking the city. He burned it to the ground in reprisal for the missing treasure and returned to Jamaica with his share of the loot, leaving the remainder of the fleet to fend for themselves. As a result of his invasion the Spanish threatened to

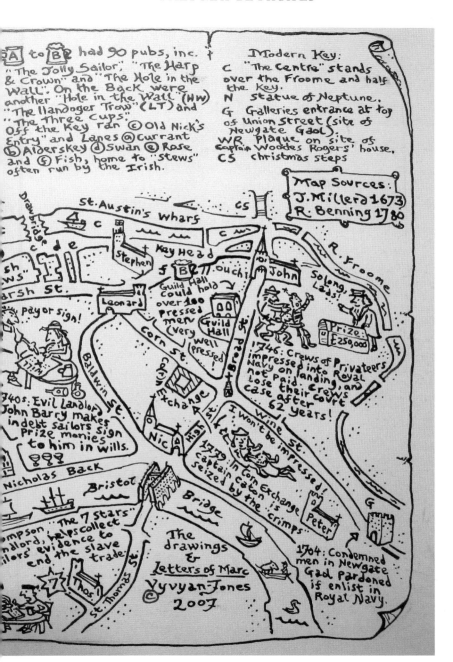

Map of the haunts of Bristol's pirates and privateers.

declare war on England, and to placate them King Charles had Morgan shipped back to England and imprisoned in the Tower of London. Despite this, as soon as things quietened down, Henry was released, knighted, and sent back to Jamaica as 'Lieutenant Governor Sir Henry Morgan'. Who says crime doesn't pay?

Bristol's other pirate, Blackbeard, wasn't so lucky. He eventually lost his head to Lieutenant Maynard of the Royal Navy who had been sent to end his depredations in the Caribbean once and for all. After a particularly bloody and protracted battle, the head of Edward Teach, aka Blackbeard, returned to his home country hanging from the bowsprit of Maynard's ship. To this day people in the Carolinas are still searching for his treasure.

Equally famous were the exploits of Woodes Rogers and William Dampier who also sailed from Bristol on their historic three-year circumnavigation of the world.

**Privateers**
Woodes Rogers, son of a West Country mariner family from Poole, lived in Queen Square (where his house is now marked by a blue plaque) and became a freeman of Bristol through his marriage to Sarah, daughter of Rear Admiral Whetstone. At one stage Rogers was a Newfoundland trader, but business losses through enemy action caused him to turn to privateering. One of the conditions for issuing Letters of Marque was 'Reprisal for Losses', which would have applied to Rogers. He took advantage of the 1702 relaxation of prize rules, at which time the Crown reduced its take to 10 per cent plus customs dues, leaving the remainder to be shared between owners and crew. With this encouragement, in 1708 he obtained funding from Bristol Merchant Venturers and fitted out what became two of the most famous privateering ships of the time, the *Duke* and the *Duchess*. The round-the-world voyage of Woodes Rogers and his navigator William Dampier has been written about many times, but one notable event on their 1708 voyage resulted in literary history. When they called at the Pacific Islands of Juan Fernandez to take on water, they discovered Alexander Selkirk, who had been marooned there over four years before by a ship from Dampier's previous expedition of 1683–91. Upon their return to Bristol, Selkirk's account of his lonely exile reached the ears of Daniel Defoe, allegedly providing him with the plot for *Robinson Crusoe*.

Rogers was offered the governorship of the Bahamas and in 1717 on behalf of the British Government he extended an amnesty to privateers who had overstepped the mark – or should we say 'Marque'? One beneficiary of this amnesty was Benjamin Hornigold, the pirate who had once given Blackbeard his start in piracy. Hornigold earned his amnesty by using his knowledge of the pirates' lairs to hunt them down for Governor Rogers.

## A Matter of Distinction

In order to put the exploits, nefarious or otherwise, of our seafaring ancestors into context it might help if we start by looking at some of the distinctions between pirates, privateers and men of war. Indeed, the definition of each has varied, depending upon the age in which the terms were used.

Was privateering always synonymous with piracy? The answer is 'sometimes'. Initially, privateers were privately owned ships fitted out to cruise against the enemy of the Crown. This has been nicely summed up by Diana and Michael Preston in their work on Dampier, in which they describe privateering as an expeditious blend of 'private profit and public patriotism'. Permission to undertake privateering was issued in the form of a Royal Commission or Letter of Marque. At the beginning of the eighteenth century, the term was 'Letter of Marque Ship', referring to the commission, but soon the word 'ship' was dropped. Confusion often arose because, although the Letter of Marque might be valid when the privateer set out, by the time it engaged with and captured an enemy ship, thus claiming it as a lawful prize, the national alliances might have changed, so the action might no longer be lawful.

A noted but tragic example of the cost of delayed news was the punishing battle between USS *Constitution* and HMS *Levant* and HMS *Cyane* that took place nine days after the news of the Treaty of Ghent (which ended the 1812–15 war between America and Great Britain) had reached New York. Often with privateers, if the potential prize looked too good to miss, news of any peace would be ignored. However, if this defiance was witnessed, the captain's action would be classed as piracy and the appropriate punishments would be meted out, or at least the prize would be confiscated, with the owners having to pay compensation to the aggrieved government. This was true unless, of course, like Henry Morgan, you made sure the King got his cut. In this way many privateers drifted into piracy or mixed the two because, of course with piracy, if you got away with it you didn't have to share the spoils with any other than your crew.

So how did the shipowners get crews for their ships? Was it skulduggery or coercion that worked best? A privateer, a pirate, a merchant seaman, a Jack Tar in the Royal Navy or a seaman on a slaver – the difference between these vessels meant that some ships' captains could advertise for crew, and select from the applicants, while other captains had to resort to violence to get seamen aboard. 'Men of war' generally referred to Royal Navy ships and, dependant upon the captain's reputation, these ships either had ready and willing applicants or had to rely on naval recruiting agents, known as 'crimps'. An unlucky captain, or one with a harsh reputation, or even when circumstances meant there was a shortage of experienced sailors such as during wartime, would need to rely on the dreaded impressment officers (usually shortened to press gang) in order to grab enough men off the streets to crew his ship. However, the press gangs were only concerned with numbers and grabbed landlubbers as well as sailors, many of whom jumped ship at the first opportunity.

**The Perils Of Debt**
In 1705 debtors in Bristol's Newgate jail were released if they agreed to enlist in the navy – or if they could persuade a substitute to enlist in their place. (For another example of substitution or official skulduggery read about a Tyburn Ticket in the chapter entitled 'Conundrums In Stone'.) A notable example of the scheme in operation can be found in the records for 1704 which contain an account of Edward Taunton who had been sentenced to death for burglary but was offered the Queen's pardon if he enlisted in the navy. In 1706 the act was extended to every debtor with assets of less than £60, who was given the opportunity to volunteer or be forced by the Magistrates to enlist – giving lie to the expression, 'a volunteer is worth ten pressed men'. Even with these draconian measures there were still insufficient men for the ships. The problem of recruitment didn't only apply to Royal Navy ships. A ship was commissioned in 1706 to protect Bristol merchants' ships from the ravages of Barbary pirates lurking in the Bristol Channel. However, in order to crew the protection ship, the

city and the Merchant Venturers had to raise £350 of bounty money in order to muster enough sailors to man the ship.

Even though in the preceding year war had been declared on France, 1745 was generally a bad year for Bristol shipowners, with the Spanish and French war ships capturing many British ships. A splendid exception can be seen in the actions of Captain Philips of the ship *Alexander* who managed to cut out from under the noses of the French a captured Royal Navy 28-gun ship of the line that they were refitting to use as an escort for their own merchant fleet, about to sail to the West Indies. Captain Philips not only managed to recover the ship intact and bring her back to Bristol as a prize, but he also brought 200 of the French crew, receiving for his endeavours a 500-guinea prize and a medal from the King.

Merchant ships came from other English ports and even as far afield as Virginia to stock up on goods at the world famous St James' Fair. For example, in the 1750s merchants such as John Norton & Sons of London and Virginia would come to Bristol and rent a warehouse for the ten days of the fair, during which time it would be gradually filled with a ship load of commodities for the new colony. Having got the goods safely onboard, and not having lost any of the crew to press gangs or other hazards of life ashore, they then had to negotiate the tides and shoals of the River Avon. Having successfully set off from the King Road there was always a risk that pirates were lying in wait for them behind Steep Holm – which was why Bristol had found it necessary to commission a protection ship for the merchants.

Despite this, even local ships had their problems with negotiating the River Avon. As revealed in Lloyd's List for 9 April 1745 the privateer *Falcon* ran aground at the Hungroad, and sank to its mast tops where it lay, completely blocking the river, for nearly a month. It remained a danger to other shipping until official action was taken to have it broken up and removed. As a result of this incident, and prompted no doubt by some pretty irate merchants, money was allocated to get the shoals removed. Yet even a century later there was a more spectacular wreck due to a combination of the tides and a non-local tug pilot unfamiliar with the hazards of the Avon. This event left its mark on Bristol in the form of a left-handed giant (see the chapter entitled 'Bizarre Beliefs and Odd Occurrences').

**Duplicity**

Privateers *Prince Frederick* and *Duke*, of the London Merchants and Captains, arrived at the King Road at the mouth of the River Avon on 8 September 1745 with treasure to the value of nearly £1 million. They had captured this from two French merchantmen encountered off the American coast, war with France having been declared the previous April. Although the Frenchmen put up a resolute fight, they surrendered when their commanders were killed. The ships' masts had been shot away, which meant that the prize had to be towed back across the Atlantic. The booty comprised over 1,000 chests of silver bullion weighing over 2.5 million ounces, as well as gold and silver wrought plate and other valuables and upon the crews' return to Bristol there were wild rejoicings in the streets. It took twenty-two wagons to transport the treasure to the Royal Mint in London and not surprisingly the convoy of wagons was provided with an armed escort of marines and sailors. The sailors, no doubt, went along so that they could keep a weather eye on their gains. The stupendous amount of the prize would mean a life of opulence for the owners and rekindle the interest in privateering ventures. However, the shares of promised riches for the crew never materialised. The sailors who had returned to Bristol were defrauded by being immediately impressed into Royal Navy ships, many with the prospect of long voyages in unhealthy conditions in front of them, with the likelihood of being either killed in action or succumbing to the many diseases before they could return to claim their promised share. This left many sailors wives and families destitute.

**Terrible Deeds In The Pothouse**

An incident that arose from this particular prize voyage uncovered another long-running fraud that had been perpetrated on the luckless sailors. The fraud came to light as a result of the tragic death of one of the heroes of the captured French prizes. James Barry, an officer on the *Duke*, whose prize share would have been about £2,000, was invited to take up shore leave residence at the Harp and Crown inn on the Quay. After only a few days in residence he suddenly died. The landlord, John Barry (no relation), submitted a will for probate saying that James had made the will in his favour just before his death. Suspicions were aroused and an investigation revealed terrible deeds.

John Barry, had for some years employed a disbarred attorney, in the vernacular a 'hedge attorney', one Peter Haynes, whose job at the inn was to 'help with the paperwork'. It seems that the landlord and his myrmidons seduced sailors into the premises with promises of cheap lodgings and beer, encouraged them to spend what money they had, which probably wasn't difficult, and then when they had no more cash, to run up a slate. The landlord knew the gullible sailors wouldn't be in a position to clear their slate when a berth on a ship called them back to sea and to clear their debt he would get them to sign their mark to a blank will form drawn up by the rascally Haynes. If they didn't agree to sign, they would be threatened with the debtors' prison – the officially sanctioned recruitment centre for the dreaded press gangs. After their departure or probable demise, the will, completed in the innkeeper's favour, would be filed. Each time the landlord successfully claimed a hapless sailor's prize money Haynes received £11 commission. In court Haynes testified that he had completed several hundred wills such as this for the landlord. It was James Barry's death that precipitated the investigation and brought matters to light. It turned out that the landlord's wife had put a pen in the dead officer's hand and made his mark upon the blank will, which was then completed by Haynes and witnessed by the inn's pot boy who had been intimidated into signing. Barry was not surprisingly found guilty, and executed on the St Michael's Hill gallows. What is not recorded is why none of the registry or court officials ever queried the number of bequests to the same beneficiary. This leaves us with an interesting question: how was it that a single person, the landlord of the Harp and Crown, was able to successfully submit hundreds wills of seamen made out in his favour, all of whom had stayed at his inn? Perhaps, as seems likely, there is another scandal hidden in this account waiting to be uncovered.

At this point it is worth noting that not all the landlords of sailors' taverns were so venal or wicked. For example, Thompson, the landlord of the Seven Stars in St Thomas parish near the Redcliffe Backs, also provided lodgings for sailors but was active in helping them find berths on other ships. He was appalled at the treatment the slave captains meted out to their crews and was instrumental in helping Reverend Thomas Clarkson, the cleric who worked with abolitionist William Wilberforce, and who gave up his church calling to actively campaign for the abolition of the buying and transporting of slaves, along with all the practices and abuses associated with slavery. (The chapter entitled 'The Five Thomases' looks at Clarkson's work in more detail.)

Had tales of similar events reached the ears of Robert Louis Stevenson; could they have been in his mind when he wrote *Treasure Island*? A conversation takes place in Chapter Nine of the novel in which Long John Silver tells the young seaman:

> About gentlemen of fortune. They lives rough, and they risks swinging, but they eat and drink like fighting cocks, and when a cruise is done, why it's hundreds of pounds instead hundreds of farthings in their pockets. Now, the most goes for rum and a good fling, and to sea again in their shirts.

Another nautical tradition associated with pirates but that also applied to sailors and fishermen was the wearing of a gold earring in the left ear. This was to provide for the cost of a decent burial should they be lost at sea and their body washed ashore.

Sailors enjoying the delights of the fleshpots and quayside pubs on their all-too brief and sometimes unpleasantly interrupted shore leaves would have probably been cheered by seeing a version of their prayer on pub walls:

> O Lord above send down a dove,
> With wings as sharp as razors,
> To cuts the throats of all those blokes
> Who sell bad beer to sailors.

A framed copy of this old prayer can be seen behind the bar in the Bristol sailors' pub, the Port of Call.

## The Royal Family

In 1746 London Merchants and Captains commissioned a further Privateering expedition that comprised ships known as 'The Royal Family' because they all had names connected with royalty. The *Prince Frederick*, the *King George*, *Princess Amelia* and the *Duke*, were all fitted out at Bristol and left the King Road on 28 April 1746, returning at the end of the year having netted nearly a quarter of a million pounds in prizes. Before sailing the crew had been promised a bounty of fifteen guineas each, but this was reduced to five guineas once they had set sail. The returning crews had hardly set foot upon dry land when they were again defrauded by what can only be assumed to have been collusion between the local impressment officers and the privateers' owners, who had them quickly rounded up and impressed onto Royal Navy ships before they could collect their prize money.

Matters were so bad that in 1749 some of the sailors filed a bill in Chancery to recover their unpaid prize money from the owners, which took three years to rule in the sailors' favour. However, legal delays went on until 1783, delayed again until 1789, then 1799 and even until the next century, by which time many of the sailors were probably dead, and their families in the poorhouse. The final insult came in the hearing of 1810 after more than sixty-two years of legal procrastination when the judges ruled that there were irregularities in the plaintiffs' paperwork and the case was thrown out. Such a situation is reminiscent of that old music hall song with the line, 'It's the rich wot gets the pleasure, and the poor wot gets the blame'.

## Biter Bit
Although the Algerian corsairs were a real menace to Bristol shipping, occasionally Bristol ships got the upper hand. One spectacular success was gained by Captain Carbry. His ship, the *Phoenix*, returning with a cargo from Spain, was captured by a 30-gun corsair. The six Turkish pirates planned to take the *Phoenix* and her crew to Algiers, where no doubt the crew would have ended their lives as galley slaves. However, the redoubtable Cabry and three of his crew managed to attack and throw overboard two of the pirates and retake the ship, arriving without further incident back at the King Road. The British Government took a sworn statement from Cabry because he had a valid passport issued by the Dey of Algiers that allowed him to trade in those waters off Lisbon where his ship was taken. The pirates justified their action claiming that the passport was a forgery.

## The Ill-Named 'Jolly Sailor'
Sometimes the exploits of the press gangs led to open warfare on the streets. On one occasion, a press gang had been tipped off, probably by the landlady or a crimp, or as the sailors would have said, 'the secret has been told to the parrot', that there were five sailors from a priva-

Jolly Sailor public house on the Quay.

teer in the Jolly Sailor pub near the quayside. The gang surrounded the pub whereupon the sailors took to the roof and fired at them. The landlady was shot in the neck by a member of the press gang while one of the privateers shot one of their own, and the rest were captured and taken off to become not so jolly Jack Tars. In theory privateersmen were exempt from the press gang, but this technicality was often overlooked by the press gang in the haste to meet their 'quota'.

## The Mighty Press Gang

The navy's press gangs became ever more brutal after receiving local government sanction to get sailors by whatever means necessary to crew their ships. With the collusion of the common council, they acted on instructions from the mayor who had been told that Bristol had to provide 500 seamen for His Majesty's Service. Ever ready to oblige, constables searched all the taverns and arrested as many sailors as they could find, over 100, and locked them up in the Guildhall, guarded by Royal Marines, until they could be taken aboard the Royal

Hole in the Wall public house, The Grove, Queen Square.

Navy ships. A couple of months later a similar exercise took place with a mixed bag of nearly 200 men being kidnapped in a single night. Bristol had the worst reputation for the depredations of the press gangs in the kingdom.

Sailors, tailors, chapmen, hatmen, irrespective of suitability or legality, all were grist to the press gang's mill. When, in 1708, Woodes Rogers and William Dampier had set off on their round-the-world voyage, they got no farther than Ireland before they had to replace over 100 of their crew who turned out to be unsuitable landlubbers. Nevertheless, the navy had a ship standing by to take the 'rejects' for their own ships.

It was in this climate of licensed kidnapping that pubs such as the Hole in the Wall on The Grove flourished (there was another of the same name in nearby Prince Street). This was because the pub had a small room much like a bay window that provided a safe lookout both ways along The Grove dockside for the dreaded press gangs, while a long passage at the rear of the pub gave the patrons an escape route into Queen Square. The original name of the pub on The Grove, dating from 1700, was the Coach and Horses. However, the pub also has an interesting literary claim to fame, one encouraged by the twentieth-century owners and the tourist industry. It is possible that the inn provided the inspiration for Robert Louis Stevenson's the Spy Glass Inn, where Jim Hawkins meets Long John Silver in *Treasure Island*.

The press gangs didn't limit their depredations to taking men and boys from off the streets. One of the most blatant abuses of the system took place towards the end of 1756 when the *Virginia Merchant*, having barely arrived back at the King Road after a year-long voyage, was boarded by a Royal Navy party intent on impressing the crew. The crew took violent exception – official reports said 'a firm resistance' – the outcome of which was that the navy tender fired upon the *Virginia Merchant* killing a crew member and injuring several others, and damaging the ship so badly that she sank. No mention was made of the fate of the rest of the crew.

The situation got so bad that the captains of the merchant ships resorted to offloading their crews before they got to the King Road, and again on their outward voyage the crew would make their way down country to be picked up by the ship's jolly boat from the Somerset coast. It was the navy's practice of stopping ships on the high seas and impressing sailors on the flimsiest of excuses that was a contributory factor in the Anglo-American war of 1812.

Ye Llandoger Trow, King Street.

### Recruitment into a life at Sea

Although these accounts may give the impression that all ships' crews were obtained by force or deception, crews for merchantmen and privateers were also recruited by advertising. For example, on 4 May 1757 a local newspaper ran an advertisement for the famous *Tyger* privateer. The notice asked for 'all officers, seaman, landsmen and others that are willing to enter on board the said privateer, let them repair to the sign of the Llandoger Trow in King Street where they will meet with proper encouragement.'

The cruise was planned to last four months, and because of her previous successes the owners probably had no difficulty in crewing her. For example, another broadsheet concerned with the paying out of prize money for the *Tyger's* first cruise read:

> This is to give notice. To the Officers, Seamen and others, belonging to the *Tyger's* first cruise, that the prize money for the ships, *Comtesse de Conflans*, *Bien Acquis* and the *Judith* taken by the said privateer will be paid them on Monday next, at Nine o'clock in the morning, at the sign of the Three Cups on the Back.

Drinking houses around Skadpule Street, which ran parallel to the Quay (the present-day Marsh Street), were dens of thieves, press gangs and crimps. If the privateers were the easiest to recruit with the sometimes-false promises of shares in the rich pickings, the Royal Navy ships had much more difficulty, mainly due to the harsh discipline, but the worst of the lot were the slave ships, those vessels taking human African cargoes to the plantations of the New World. The stews and pothouses of Skadpule Street, run mainly by Irishmen, were frequented by the mates who lured young sailors with promises of high wages, and when they were in their cups, enticed them onto the ships' jolly boats kept waiting at the quayside. When they had a boatload, they were taken to the slave ship moored in the Hungroad. If the mates' blandishments were insufficient to lure the sailor to the jolly boat, the other technique was to get them drunk into insensibility, and the hapless sailor had a very rude awakening – often finding himself on the way to the open sea. The chances of him ever seeing his home again were pretty slim. Another technique employed by the slavers to get recruits was for the ship's mate to strike a deal with the landlord of the pothouse to blackmail sailors.

They were invited to take up lodgings as well as drink there. They were encouraged to drink beyond their means, and run into debt and were then threatened with prison, which was a direct route onto a Royal Navy ship. Their only way out was to sign on to a slaver voyage with promises of a share of the profits. More often than not they weren't allowed to read the ship's articles before signing (even if they could read) and when at sea, they discovered that they had agreed to a host of other clauses, such as paying for their slops or being paid in worthless local currency. All of this meant that in reality they were slaves as much as the human cargo they were transporting from Africa to the colonies.

**Please don't go to the fair Daddy!**
Press gangs (and 'crimps', see the chapter entitled 'Odd Trades'), who were always on the lookout for likely victims to lure onto Royal Navy ships really excelled themselves during the day of 12 July 1779 at a time when local merchants were assembled in the Exchange, Corn Street. A press gang entered and seized a retired sea captain and shipowner, Mr James Caton. Magistrates, who of course would themselves have been members of the business community, were incensed by the behaviour of the press gang and granted a writ of *Habeus Corpus*. This was followed up by Edmund Burke complaining to the Admiralty and, as a result, after only a few days Caton was released and successfully sued the commander of the press gang for £150 in damages. However, another example of the excessive zeal shown by the press gang was at a fair, one of their more lucrative hunting grounds. A side-show barker was using a 'Merry Andrew' (buffoon), as a warm-up man for the crowd. The press gang snatched him off the stage and carried him off, never to be seen again, leaving behind a grieving wife and starving children. Cynically one could suggest that, due to his more lowly status in society, his plight was ignored: unlike Caton, he wasn't important enough to receive judicial and parliamentary support.

**A Gruesome Afterthought**
So what actually happened to Blackbeard's disembodied skull? Did it ever return to its birthplace of Bristol and is it still in use today in some secret drinking club hidden away in a dockside haunt? If so, one wonders what terrible and bloodthirsty toasts are made – perhaps it is best not to know!

# 6

## SHIPSHAPE AND BRISTOL FASHION

This is the expression that Bristol has given the world and it is generally taken, whether at sea or on dry land, to indicate a state of tidiness and a well-run enterprise. Although Bristolians are flattered that it has become a worldwide figure of speech, the expression means more than just tidiness and has a sound and pragmatic basis, going back to when Bristol was a staple port and the second city in the country outside London. The pragmatic origin of the expression explains why, in the days of exploration, sailors from Bristol were so successful. Remember the voyages of Canynge, Cabot, Jay, James, Pring, Hawkins, Rogers and Dampier, not forgetting the many others such as Morgan and Blackbeard whose voyages were of a more nefarious nature but still owed their success to sailing in Bristol-built ships? The reason for this was that the expression 'Ship Shape and Bristol Fashion' was an example of how to make a virtue out of necessity. While accepting that it was an acknowledgement of Bristol's maritime expertise, what may not be obvious is the fact that this expertise was born from Bristol shipbuilders' need to accommodate their designs to suit the town's unique topographical situation.

The city and port straddles the tidal River Avon several miles upriver from the mouth, which opens into the Severn estuary. It is the funnelling effect of the Severn estuary, forcing the tidal water upstream to Bristol that is responsible for the city having the second highest tides in the world. One effect of these tidal extremes on the medieval shipbuilders was the need to construct ships that could withstand being left high and dry twice a day. This led to the building of very strong ships, which meant that explorers sailing in Bristol ships had a higher survival rate. In other words, Bristol explorers could sail further and, equally importantly, they generally returned to tell the tale. But what about the 'tidiness'? If your ship, when in port, was going to be lying on its side for a good part of each 24-hour cycle, everything needed to be well stowed and tidily put away. (This trait has become part of the Bristolian psyche; a recent survey revealed that more Bristol men hang up their clothes when going to bed than any others in Britain.) The shipboard tidiness also meant that storms at sea were more likely to be survived.

Bristol's maritime fame as a result of this shipbuilding skill was evident from the time of the Saxon Chronicles when Harold and Leofwine were able to escape from the clutches of Edward the Confessor by sailing to Ireland in a Bristol boat. It carries on down the ages, past all the explorers, until we reach the nineteenth century, when Isambard Kingdom Brunel chose Bristol as the location at which to build the first paddle steamer that successfully crossed the Atlantic, followed by the first and largest screw-driven iron ship in the world. Sadly it was Bristol's success that provided the impetus to build bigger and bigger ships, which in turn saw the unique topographical situation become a commercial millstone around the neck of the port.

Bristol ships could withstand the rigours of exploration, which brought prosperity to the town, but the same feature that benefited the early explorers became a terrible liability in later centuries when the city needed to exploit their discoveries. The first proposals to over-come the tidal limitation were to 'dockise' the river, which involved fitting lock gates across the river so that once through, the ships could remain afloat irrespective of the tides. This system also included a canal bypass for the river flow. Although it took years of wrangling, numerous proposals, which included fitting lock gates at various places along the reach of the Avon, finally resulted in the building of the Floating Harbour. The proposed locations ranged from where they are today at Cumberland Basin, down to the Hungroad at Shirehampton, and even down at the river mouth.

However, it was another aspect of the topography that finally did for the port as a city centre location, and that was the Avon's tortuous route. As soon as ships started getting larger in the nineteenth century, they experienced increasing difficulty in negotiating the river's bends and tides. At the time of spring tides and storms, the river saw a veritable log jam of ships, and on one black day as many as eight were either stranded or wrecked along the length of the river. Finally, by the time the authorities had got their act together, figuratively and in parlia-mentary terms, a lot of the trade had moved to Liverpool or even across the channel to Cardiff and Swansea. Only then did the port authorities see reason and move the port first to Avonmouth, and then with the advent of even bigger container ships, to Portbury Wharf on the south bank of the river mouth.

Nevertheless the expression lives on, and although the shipbuilding has now, apart from specialist yards, all but ceased, there are still many ships plying the world's oceans that are emblazoned with a badge bearing the proud words 'Shipshape and Bristol fashion'. This came about because one of Bristol's most successful shipbuilding and shipping dynasties, that of Charles Hill and Sons, decided during the Second World War to adopt the local expression as their house badge and thereafter had a badge with the motto fitted to each of the ships built by them. The company had been started by James Hillhouse in the early eighteenth century and was joined by Charles Hill in 1810 who, in the fullness of time, became a partner. When George Hillhouse (son of James) retired from active business it became known as Hillhouse and Hill (at that time George was still the overall owner). In the middle of the century Charles took over the business completely, at which time it became known as Charles Hill and Sons. The last ship to wear the badge was the 1,500-ton *Miranda Guinness*, which was launched from the Albion Dockyard, inside Bristol's Floating Harbour, at the end of 1976.

Although there is no connection with either the City of Bristol or with ships, the spirit of the expression 'Shipshape and Bristol Fashion' was adopted by the first owners of a worldwide chain of luxury hotels. The proprietors felt that the name was synonymous with a degree of togetherness, smartness and tidiness that portrayed the image they wanted people to associate with their world famous 'Bristol Hotels'.

Lastly, when we were a predominately maritime nation, we also gave the world another nautical expression, 'copper bottomed', meaning a ship that was clad below the water line with copper sheets to keep the dreaded teredo worm at bay, which gnawed its way through ship's hulls and was responsible for the loss of many a ship and her crew. Another benefit of copper-bottomed ships was that they did not attract so much weed and barnacles, and so could travel further without needing to be careened and cleaned. Thus a 'copper-bottomed ship' meant a lower insurance risk and a better investment for the captain's merchant backers, leading to the phrase 'a copper bottomed-investment'. Not surprisingly, in order to service the city's many shipyards Bristol had its own copper nail and sheathing company. The company issued its own tokens (copper of course), and, the larger penny token for the 'British Copper Company of Walthamstow and Landore' (Swansea) dated 1812, and the other smaller half penny token issued by the 'Bristol Patent Sheathing Nail Manufactory, Payable at Bristol & London'.

As an aside, tokens such as these were issued by companies as wages but generally could only be used in the company store, a widely used but restrictive practice that was even mentioned much later in a Johnny Cash song. In England this practice was abolished by the nineteenth-century Parliamentary Truck Act, which forced employers to pay their employees the full amount of their wages in cash, although this was modified again as recently as 1960 by the Payment of Wages Act, which enabled employers to pay wages directly into employees' bank accounts.

# 7

## A FATEFUL DECISION

The day that the son of a Bristol sugar baker (the process in which rough sugar imported to Bristol was converted from cane pulp into lump sugar) decided to use his initiative to help the merchants of Hamburg turned out to be an initiative that reverberated down the centuries and resulted in the birth of a London tradition. Francis Freeling was born on 25 August 1764 at 24 Redcliffe Hill, Bristol, and attended the neighbourhood Pile Street School (the same school where the boy poet, Thomas Chatterton's father was schoolmaster). He was later educated at Colston's School and upon leaving joined the Bristol Post Office as a trainee. In those days the Post Office was in the building on the corner of Exchange Avenue and Corn Street. Nowadays this site is occupied by a travel agency but the Post Office name is still visible where it was cut into the stonework above the corner window. Even as an apprentice, the application, talent and honesty of young Francis soon drew him to the attention of his superiors. As a result, his first opportunity soon came when he was made

The old Post Office building in Bristol, where Francis Freeling started work.

assistant to John Palmer, inventor and promoter of a network of fast mail coaches. In order to understand how Freeling came to be in the position to make the fateful decision it will help to look at the formative events in his career.

When he moved to Bath as Palmer's chief assistant, this was Freeling's first move, both up the career ladder and away from Bristol. Freeling supported Palmer in his fight for the introduction of fast and dependable armed coaches, which in those lawless days gave the mail a much better chance of actually arriving at its destination. Prior to this, the mail had been carried by a system of unarmed 'boy' messengers (often old men), which resulted in high losses of both postboys and mail. Attacks on the armed mail coaches were infrequent, thanks to Palmer and Freeling's initiative in providing armed guards. Although robberies still took place, in the main these were limited to the vicinity of coaching inns or other stops. However, a notable incident outside the Post Office's control took place on 20 October 1816. This happened when the Exeter to London mail had just left Salisbury and was approaching the Pheasant Inn, at Winterslow, on the road to Stockbridge (now the A30). One of the leading horses in the team was attacked and dragged down by an escaped lion. The passengers fled to the safety of the inn, except for one panic-stricken man who didn't make it in time and was locked out. Although the lioness was recaptured and the man survived to write up the momentous event for the local papers, it obviously preyed upon his mind, because he became an incurable lunatic, living out the remainder of his days in the local asylum at Laverstock.

Palmer and Freeling's next innovation was the introduction of a system of cross mail coaches. Before this, to get a letter from Bristol to Portsmouth it had to go from Bristol along the Great West Road to London. Then, if it arrived, it had to be transferred to another coach to Portsmouth. The advent in 1785 of a direct Bristol to Portsmouth service was the first of the new 'cross routes', and its success paved the way for many more cross routes, thus breaking the London monopoly on the mail system. As with many innovations, opposition came from vested interests that had benefited from the opportunities offered by long and costly routes.

Yet from these modest beginnings Freeling was soon promoted to the main office in London where he eventually rose to become

Secretary General of the Post Office, during which time he introduced many improvements to the mail service. However, to set the scene for the next part of the story we need to travel back to the time of the Fench Revolutionary Wars in the Mediterranean.

The year 1793 witnessed the execution of Louis XVI of France and saw Napoleon Bonaparte's first success at the Battle of Toulon, home of France's main Mediterranean naval base forty-two miles southeast of Marseilles. During this battle Napoleon distinguished himself by successfully attacking both the British and Spanish. However, it was not a complete success for him, because amongst the ships he lost was a frigate called the *Sprite* (*La Lutine*). The ship was one of a number captured by the Royal Navy; on 18 December she was one of sixteen ships handed over by French royalists to the British fleet under the command of Vice-Admiral Lord Hood. In 1795, she was rebuilt as a fifth-rate frigate with 38 guns and renamed *Lutine*. Frigates acted as fast scouts or independent cruisers with a crew of about 250. These postings were sought after due to their manoeuvrability and firepower, which meant that they were often assigned to interdict enemy shipping with the likelihood that they would acquire prize money.

The weather in the summer of 1799 was appalling and this, combined with the effect of the blockade of European ports meant that trade with the continent was at a virtual standstill with serious economical consequences for Britain's European allies. To avert the threat of imminent bankruptcy from the Hamburg Merchant allies, the Bank of England decided to support them by sending a large shipment of gold and silver bullion. Because this was to be shipped via the Post Office Royal Mail packet ships, the General Secretary of the Post Office, at that time Francis Freeling, would have been responsible for its safe transfer with the preferred route to the continent being from Yarmouth to Cuxhaven.

However, there was a problem. Because of the blockade and bad weather the East Coast packet boats hadn't been able to sail and at Yarmouth there was a backlog of mail, parcels and passengers. It was then that Francis Freeling made the crucial decision. No doubt pressured by his superiors to find some way of getting the all-important funds to the Hamburg Merchants, he looked for an alternative means of transporting the bullion, reported to be between £1 million and £1.25 million (reports vary).

Our story now comes back to the *Lutine*. Since her capture, she had been used in the North Sea, and along the north coast of Holland, specifically the area of the Waddenzee, on patrol and escort duties. But what was important was that Yarmouth was now her home port and, moreover, in that fateful October she had just returned there from Southampton. Here was the obvious answer to Frances Freeling's transport problem: a Royal Navy frigate in port, with a crew under the command of Captain Lancelot Skynner, experienced in the North Holland coastal waters. Freeling therefore personally ordered that the bullion to be taken to Cuxhaven by *Lutine*. Thus, on 9 October 1799 *Lutine* set sail for Holland with the bullion that was to restore our allies' finances. Disaster! The *Lutine* never made it to Holland. The ship sank between the Dutch Friesian Islands of Terschelling and Vlieland with only one survivor. As with the value of the bullion, accounts of the causes of the sinking vary. These range from appalling weather, a storm which drove the ship onto a lee shore, and retribution by the French who sank her. There are also a few conspiracy theories.

At the end of the war the ownership of the wrecked ship was formally handed over by the Dutch Government to the Corporation of Lloyd's who had insured the cargo. Over the years there have been a number of salvage attempts. In 1859 the wreck yielded its most important treasure – the 48 kg, 46 cm diameter ship bell. This was hung in Lloyd's underwriting room at the Royal Exchange in London and a tradition grew up for it to be rung when news of overdue ships arrived. Whenever a vessel became overdue underwriters would ask specialist brokers to reinsure some of their liability based upon the possibility of the ship becoming a total loss. As soon as reliable information about the safe arrival, or the loss of the ship, became available the ringing of the bell ensured that everyone with an interest in the risk became aware of the news simultaneously.

Nowadays, the 'Lutine Bell' is rung on ceremonial occasions and on the, thankfully, rare instances of major loss of life. For example, the bell was tolled following the terrorist attacks on 11 September 2001.

Another salvage attempt was made in 1886 when one of the *Lutine*'s thirty-eight cannon, was recovered from beneath sand in over fifty feet of water and Lloyd's were able to present it to Her Majesty Queen Victoria, who accepted the gift and had it transferred to the battlements of Windsor Castle.

So the series of events set in motion by Francis Freeling's fateful but probably unavoidable decision on 9 October 1799 to entrust to the *Lutine* the most important bullion shipment of his career resulted in the introduction of a maritime tradition that continues today, over 200 years later.

It is also nice to be able to report that those in authority recognised that although the decision had been his, the circumstances that lost the ship had been outside his control and on another occasion he was asked to transport an even more nationally valuable cargo than that ill-fated bullion. On 12 August 1821 the steam packet *Lightning* transported George IV to Ireland. To mark the voyage and the occasion of the King's birthday he presented an engraved tortoiseshell and gold snuff box to Freeling. His proud granddaughter, Edith Freeling, remembered that the selection of this particular item as a royal gift indicated a knowledge of Francis Freeling's tastes, as at this time he was building up a significant personal collection of snuff boxes and by the time of his death had over seventy.

The culmination of Francis Freeling's postal career came on 11 March 1828. It was then that Queen Victoria decided to honour him, in recognition of the many improvements and innovations that over the years he had successfully introduced to the Royal Mail postal service, by bestowing a baronetcy on him. What a pity that no memorial exists to him in his native city other than his memorial plaque in the church of St Mary Redcliffe where he was buried. However, the good news is that when the Royal Mail moved its archives from Freeling House in Glasshouse Street, London, to its new premises, they continued to honour his memory by naming their new building Freeling House.

Sir Francis Freeling Bart., FSA, lived out the remainder of his life in London, and died at his home in Bryanston Square in July 1836. Here in his native city of Bristol, apart from his postal legacy, we also have, thanks to the fame of that other Redcliffe boy, poet Thomas Chatterton, another memory of Francis Freeling's relatively short time in Bristol. Mr Dix, writing about Chatterton, mentioned that when the young Chatterton was making his farewells to his Bristol family and friends on the steps of St Mary Redcliffe Church before setting off for London, he went over the way to Mr Freeling's house, Mr Freeling being the father of Francis. Also, we are thankful to Mr

Tombs, who wrote the key works on the history and development of the Post Office in Bristol, and indicating on a picture of Redcliffe Hill the location of Francis's house at No. 24 (it is marked with a cross). The drawing by Delamotte in 1831 annotated on the back in Freeling's own handwriting is now in the possession of the City Museum and Art Gallery.

Freeling inspired a number of people during his long career with the Post Office, not least of which was the writer Anthony Trollope, who started his literary career as a clerk in the Post Office under his tutelage.

Lastly, to learn about another tradition associated with the ringing of the Lutine Bell we have to go to the Abbotsbury Swannery in Dorset. The current swanherd, Dave Wheeler, explained that since 1837 their Mute Swans have provided the quill feathers for the pen that is used to make entries in the Loss Book at Lloyd's Registry (although in some years this was also known as the Loss and Casualty Book), a tradition that continues to this day. Interestingly, when Lloyd's started the Loss Book in 1837 swan quills would have been the norm for good quality writing instruments, and it was only later in the century with the advent of steel-nibbed pens and then fountain pens (or more correctly, self-filling pens), that using a quill to make loss entries became special. Wheeler's predecessor, John Fair (1975–95), and before him Fred Lexster from the 1950s, all provided quills to Lloyd's for the Loss Book entries. Wheeler also explained that, with the increased interest in calligraphy, perhaps as a reaction to ball-point pen writing, they now have a challenge meeting the demand. This is because the specific feathers used for quill pens are the primary feathers from the Mute Swan, which can only be collected in the summer when they are moulted by the swans on the nest site. In addition to calligraphers they are also asked to supply quills to fletchers (for arrow flights) and to beekeepers (for brushing bees off combs).

In conclusion it is interesting to note that the bell recovered from *Lutine* still hangs in the rostrum of the underwriting room at Lloyd's. It bears on its bronze side the crown and royal arms of the House of Bourbon, and on the rim the name of 'Saint Jean' under whose protection the ship and crew had been placed when she was launched as *La Lutine*, a fighting frigate of His Majesty, Louis XVI of France. When the ship was captured from the French by Admiral

Hood, St Jean obviously decided not to extend her protection to the Republican forces of Napoleon Bonaparte.

# 8

# OUR MISSING ANGEL

## A Trend-Setting Landmark

This particular angel was a famous Bristol landmark that watched over the people crossing Bristol Bridge or even going into the Scholastic Trading Company on the opposite side of the High Street. One of its most memorable images was the view that featured in the 1940 edition of Reece Winstone's series of photographic journals of Bristol in which it was looking over the shoulder of an *Evening World* newspaper seller.

That spot, at the High Street end of St Nicholas Church, was the newspaper seller's regular pitch. Standing six feet high, the bronzed cast-iron angel held a bible open at the book of St John, with the left-hand page showing chapter 4 verse 13: 'Whosoever drinketh of this water shall thirst again' with the right-hand page showing verse 14: 'But whosoever drinketh of the water that I shall give him shall never thirst...'. The angel, created by 'moral fervour' and nineteenth-century philanthropy, was a fountain that remained a famous Bristol landmark until it was damaged when the church was bombed during the Second World War and the surviving torso was removed for safekeeping. It was never to be seen in public again (the torso was last seen in the Industrial Museum store). Nowadays the only sign that it ever existed is the faint outline of the marble backing plate that, with the eye of faith – what else would one need to see an angel – can still be seen on the end wall of the church.

## Driven to Drink

Until the ready availability and fashion for soft drinks and bottled water, most of our non-alcoholic street refreshment came courtesy of municipal fountains. Even in the late 1950s there were dozens of drinking fountains around the city, each with their tin-plated copper drinking cup, attached by a chain. (Hereford may have its chained library, but Bristol had its chained refreshments!) Surprisingly most of the fountains date from the same year – 1859. The explanation is quite simple, but nevertheless reveals an interesting aspect of Bristol's

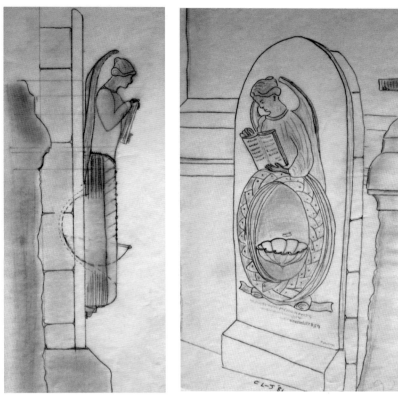

Drawings of the Angel Fountain in its former glory, as seen from the side
(*above left*) and the front (*above right*).
The sad remainder of today's Angel Fountain (*below*).

history. Prior to the provision of a city-wide municipal water supply, clean water was a luxury enjoyed by only a few, with the majority of the populace having to rely upon water from shallow wells or even from water carriers at tuppence a bucket. In theory if people paid the water carrier, or lederer, to collect water for them, it was expected, and hoped that it would be fetched from one of the half-dozen clean monastic conduit systems and that the said lederers hadn't saved themselves time and a wait in a queue at the Abbey conduit by just dipping it out of the poisonous river! This lethal practice sometimes came about because the use of the Abbey water system was controlled by the Dean of Bristol Cathedral, who only allowed the conduit tap to be turned on for a limited period each day for the parishioners' use.

Contrast their behaviour with that of the Church of St John on the Wall, whose parishioners had been granted a free branch pipe by the Carmelite Friars. The parishioners of St John's had enjoyed clear water from the springs that rose on Brandon Hill, which was piped in tunnels beneath Park Street ever since 1367.

Bristol was one of the national cholera blackspots, and the poorer districts were subjected to repeated outbreaks of the disease. The re-infections were not surprising when you discover that situations such as the following example were the norm. In Temple parish one household relied on a well that was only fifty feet away from the churchyard where cholera victims were being buried. Situations like this, together with the proximity of cesspits, explain why the water from wells often proved to be lethal.

The situation became so bad that pressure from people such as Dr William Budd, physician to the Bristol Royal Infirmary whose comment 'that the filthy habits of the poor were mainly attributable to a deficient supply of water, coupled with the fact that cholera, typhoid and related diseases were taking a terrible toll of Bristol's population, forced the government into appointing a Royal Commission to report on the health of towns, and to investigate and propose ways of improving the health of the general population. As expected from William Budd's comments, the Bristol submission for the report made horrifying reading. Their findings confirmed William Budd's comments and were summed up in Sir Henry de la Beche's and Dr L. Playfair's observations that there were 'few if any large towns in England in which the [water] supply is as inadequate as Bristol's'. They confirmed that the city's rivers were open sewers and it was generally recognised that it was safer to drink beer than water. Yet out of this damning report came the eventual establishment of a municipal water supply for everyone, not just the favoured few.

A study of Bristol's eighteenth-century inns and alehouses carried out by Williams and McGrath in the 1970s showed that by the mid-eighteenth century there were nearly a thousand ale houses, licensed or otherwise, in central Bristol. This meant that those who hadn't succumbed to cholera often fell victim to alcoholism, a situation made even worse by the 1830 Beer Act that had liberalised the licensing laws. This was also at a time when Bristol's industrial base was growing, and to meet the demand Bristol's employers needed a sober workforce. It was probably their acceptance of the problem that inspired local merchants and leaders of the business community to take action. Local business people recognised that it would not be possible to prevent alcoholism unless there was an alternative to alcoholic drink, and so they came up with the idea of providing public fountains that could be supplied from the new municipal water mains which, thanks to an Act of Parliament, came into being on 16 July 1846. This business initiative also accorded with the aims of the growing Temperance Movement. A particular branch of the Temperance Movement that targeted the young was the Band of Hope – this was at a time when even children were given beer to drink as a staple part of their diet. One of the mottoes of the Band of Hope was 'Save the child and save the nation'.

### A Solution at Last

Bristol's new water supply made people realise how bad the old systems had been and this, together with the publication of further health reports, resulted in mounting pressure from the public to get something done about the problems. However, although there was much talk, in practical terms nothing much happened until some key correspondence on the subject between Robert Laing and William Naish, Chairman of the Local Board of Health, was published in the *Bristol Times*. The newspaper report said that during a Council meeting Robert Laing had proposed that a number of free public drinking fountains should be erected around the city, and that he had offered to back up his noble sentiments with hard cash. Having made his proposal public, he was as good as his word and immediately opened a fund by putting £100 down on the table, and by the end of the year many other businessmen had followed his good example and pledged to fund public drinking-water fountains around the city.

**An Angel Arrives**
On 19 November 1859, a drinking-water fountain in the form of a cast-iron angel on a fine white marble surround was erected on the east end of St Nicholas Church. By all accounts the official opening was a splendid affair and would have shown the working classes that their need for a safe water supply had been met and that at last a source of liquid refreshment was freely available that didn't require a visit to the nearest alehouse. Understandably the promoters of the local Temperance Movement would also have been pleased by this public-spirited development. However, one wonders what their reaction must have been when they realised that the promoters and backers of the scheme followed the opening ceremony by going into the vestry of the church to congratulate themselves on their public spiritedness and to celebrate the new water fountain with a champagne lunch! Among those attending were Robert Goss, Vice Chairman of the local Board of Health, Reverend H. Martin, vicar of the parish and, of course, Robert Laing, whose generosity had started the enterprise. Other guests at the champagne lunch would have included Mr Tiley, the stonemason responsible for the marble backing and the inscription, and whose other works were within sight of the angel fountain just across the bridge in Victoria Street, together with representatives of the 'Iron Merchants of this City' who had donated the angel fountain.

At the time most Bristolians would have thought that their angel was unique; it wasn't. Although the fountain was 'top of the range' it had been selected from a Coalbrookdale Iron Works catalogue. Ever since their successful displays at the Great Exhibition of 1851, decorative cast iron in the form of seats, railings, balconies and fountains had been very much in vogue, and municipalities could browse through their catalogues and select products to adorn their streets and parks. Many fine examples of Coalbrookdale decorative cast-iron work can still be seen in and around Bristol. The 'Angel Fountain', Coalbrookdale pattern 101, was one of their finest and although Bristol has sadly 'lost' hers, another to the same pattern can still be seen in Birmingham, set in the churchyard wall of St Philip's Cathedral.

Back in the 1980s Mr Miller, a long retired Police Constable, who used to do point duty on the High Street/Baldwin Street corner remembered using the fountain. When doing point duty he used to hang his cape on the railings, and often had a drink there afterwards. Who knows, one day, especially in light of the latest announced plan to revamp Castle Park including High Street, the opportunity may arise to restore 'our missing angel' to its former glory.

But what of the very first fountain donated by Robert Laing? It was of another Coalbrookdale design, sculpted by the Wills Brothers of London, and was situated at the end of the Triangle. Sadly this too was lost during the war. Some of the others erected in that year were the 'Victoria' fountain, inset in the St Nicholas Street wall of the market (donated by the wholesale grocer, John Payne Budgett), one in Old King Street, another on St Philip's Bridge (the halfpenny bridge), and yet another on Welsh Back. In the following year one was erected in Bath Street, and from then until the end of the century merchants and local communities continued to fund them all around the city and in the new suburbs. It is a pleasure to be able to end this short account by saying that the tradition started by Robert Laing continues today, with one of the most delightful and modern designs in Bristol being that of Kate Malone's fish fountain in Castle Park.

# 9

## THE MAN WHO BOUGHT TIME...
## AND OTHER HOROLOGICAL BREAKTHROUGHS

Bristol has always been a haven for the curious – remember Cabot? And what about Henri Coanda, another famous person who brought his bump of curiosity to Bristol. Coanda played a key role in establishing Bristol's aeronautical reputation. Born in Romania in 1886 where he is recognised as the pioneer of Romanian aviation, he came to Bristol as a young man and became Technical Director for Sir George White's Bristol and Colonial Aeroplane Company at Filton. During his time working for White he designed the Bristol-Coanda aeroplanes, one of which won first prize at the International Military Aviation Contest held in England. It was for one of his discoveries as an aeronautical scientist that his name was given to the aerodynamic surface phenomena – the Coanda Effect. After a long life during which he was lauded for his scientific discoveries he eventually returned to Romania in 1970 and died there on 25 November 1972.

Bristol's inhabitants have, through the years, established a reputation for capitalising on their sense of curiosity. Another name for this ability is entrepreneurship, a term most assuredly applicable to the man who bought time. Although the title of this chapter describes yet another example of English eccentricity and determination, before naming the man in question it will probably help to explain the background to the statement. It concerns an aspect of Bristol's innovative approach to engineering that reached its apotheosis in the nineteenth century – the development of timekeeping systems.

Before the days of the fast mail coaches the routine of secular life was mainly determined by whether it was day or night and, for a given season, whether the sun was overhead or low down in the sky. Geoffrey Chaucer's character in the *Canterbury Tales* further refined time of day information by considering the length his shadow cast on the ground. In the Middle Ages most people's first introduction to mechanical forms of timekeeping would have been limited to hearing the toll of a bell in the tower of a church or, more likely, that of a monastic house. The bells were tolled by hand to mark the canonical hours of the seven monastic offices – matins, prime, terce, sext, nones, vespers and compline. The first signs of automation came in the thirteenth century when mechanical devices such as those at Westminster, Cothele and Salisbury were used to strike a bell, or bells, at the appropriate hour. As these mechanisms had no dial we often do not consider them to be clocks as such. But these early mechanical clocks needed no dial because their only function was as an alarm to automatically sound a bell to warn the sacristan of his impending duties at each canonical hour. Technically a timepiece has a dial and one or more hands, whereas a clock merely strikes a bell, as that in a clock tower.

So what, you may ask, has this to do with the man who bought time? In Bristol, as elsewhere across the country until the nineteenth century when the use of what we now recognise as clocks became widespread, time was determined by the position of the sun. When the journey to London took a day or more, the average traveller would not have noticed that the sun rose over London nearly eleven minutes before it summoned Bristolians to another day's toil. There matters would have remained but for the innovation, firstly of the rapid mail coaches that 'brought London time with them' (often in the form of a 'mail coach chronometer'), and later on by the introduction of the railways. However, it was the opening of Brunel's Great Western Railway, GWR, on 30 January 1841 that sounded the death knell for the old ways of timekeeping. This was particularly true in Bristol five months later, when on 30 June, 'God's Wonderful Railway' reached the city.

## Not Enough Time

What excitement the new railway brought, and what upset. Some of the local dignitaries had undoubtedly set their watches by the Exchange clock and set off in plenty of time to reach Brunel's spanking new railway station at Temple Meads only to discover, much to their embarrassment, that the first through train from London had arrived nearly eleven minutes beforehand! This embarrassing situation would never have arisen if it had not been for a boardroom wrangle two years before. In 1839 Wheatstone and Cooke's new system for transmitting messages by electrical telegraphy had already been installed alongside Brunel's Great Western Railway track between London and Slough, and Brunel planned to extend the system to Bristol. However, a not-sovisionary or farsighted director of the company voted against the tele-graphic system saying that it was a, 'short-lived fad that would serve no practical purpose'. It is interesting to note that it was Brunel's ship the *Great Eastern* that was used to lay the telegraph cable across the Atlantic Ocean. As a result of the director's clever decision Bristol had to wait another thirteen years to get the benefits of 'instant messaging'.

The railways formally adopted Greenwich Mean Time, GMT (or as they called it, 'Railway Time'), on 22 September 1847. But the time discrepancies weren't really highlighted until the Great Exhibition of 1851, the event that brought people flooding into London by rail from all corners of the country and the contemporary issue of *Bradshaw*, the railway travellers' bible, contained the terse note, that east–west travel was quicker than west–east travel.

## A Curious Compromise

It was mainly the business community who needed to be commercial-ly aware of London or Greenwich Mean Time, even though they were working and living in local time some ten minutes and twenty-three seconds behind. The answer, it seems, was obvious: fit the Exchange clock with two minute hands, one for local time and one for London time. Bristolians lived with this ingenuous compromise until February

The Exchange clock, complete with two minute hands.

1852 when the directors realised that perhaps electrical telegraphy might not be just a passing fad and agreed to allow the lines to be extended to Bristol. By September that year, under pressure from the business community, the Bristol Corporation agreed to formally change over to GMT, even though it still hadn't been ratified nationally by an Act of Parliament.

Although this harmonisation of time pleased most of Bristol's business people, it raised other issues. During the debates on whether Bristol should anticipate parliamentary decree, many strong words were spoken and some of the arguments against were obviously based upon conservatism (with a small c) rather than rationale. Consider the scion of the business community who stood, legs astride, in the middle of the main hall of the Commercial Rooms, pulled out of his pocket his grandfather's turnip watch and roared out 'one hand was good enough for my grandfather and it is certainly good enough for me'. (Perhaps he would have been happier living in Conningsby in Lincolnshire where the church clock only has a single hand.) The correspondence columns of the local newspapers became full of complaints, some serious, some petulant, raised by those experiencing problems, real or hypothetical, caused not by the time difference itself, but by the fact that time-dependant decisions or activities in Bristol were subject to legislative discrepancies between local bye-laws and Parliament. Two of the many examples reported include the query: 'If there is an election and I arrive at the polling station five minutes after it has closed, in accordance with Bristol adopted GMT I am disenfranchised, whereas according to the law of the land, the polling station should not shut for another five minutes and twenty-three seconds.' The other example, contained in a letter from a vicar, related to the limitation on times allowed for weddings to take place, or maybe non-weddings, because of the discrepancy between Bristol's adoption of GMT and canonical times (the clock on St Nicholas Church was changed to GMT on Saturday 18 September 1852). The vicar raised the problem caused by a couple who presented themselves five minutes after the allowable time for a wedding, according to Bristol's adoption of GMT. According to Parliament he should allow the wedding, although with only five minutes and twenty-three second remaining, they would have had to gabble their wedding vows and hope the best man didn't drop the ring! The vicar asked if the Corporation would 'cover any legal costs incurred in defending his actions'.

However, these are probably just newspaper examples of people's resistance to change. In Bristol the most vituperative and picturesque comment was from a correspondent who wrote that 'Modern legislation will sneer at the sun itself'.

In order to forestall any queries as to why the Exchange clock still has two minute hands (no it hasn't been stolen from Conningsby), a word of explanation is necessary. GMT was not adopted nationally by an Act of Parliament until 1880 when it placed all of Britain within a single time zone, at which point the second minute hand was no longer needed and it was removed. But in the early 1990s Bristol City authorities decided to reinstate it. The main clock was about to be restored and they thought that reinstating this novel feature would be a nice tourist attraction. The Temple Local History Group, who had earlier carried out a survey of the city's public clocks on behalf of the Civic Society, were asked to help with the restoration. They were able to provide the horologist with a drawing showing the 62-degree angle at which the hand should be fixed to indicate the time difference between local and GMT. The great day arrived and the restored Exchange clock was unveiled complete with its additional minute hand. But both hands were painted red and the cry went up: 'Which hand points to the right time?' This was a case of déjà vu right back to 30 June 1841, the day the dignitaries missed the train. To resolve the problem, at the official opening – or 'starting' – of the clock a few days later, the Lady Lord Mayor, Kathleen Mountstevens, armed with a can of paint and a brush, was invited to ascend in a hydraulic lift to repaint one of the minute hands a different colour. An explanatory signboard was then erected outside the Exchange to explain to mystified passers-by the reason for this horological conundrum. This possibly makes it the only clock in the country where in order to determine the time you have to read the explanatory notes beforehand (please excuse the unintentional pun)!

## Bristol Gets the Message

When the telegraph lines from London finally reached Bristol in February 1852 a temporary telegraph office was set up in an apartment in the Commercial Rooms in Corn Street, at that time the main businessmen's club, situated diagonally across the road from the Exchange. Originally proposed as a Commercial Coffee Rooms in

1808 it was established by shareholders and opened in 1811 and rapidly became the main meeting place for the city's merchants.

Not everyone benefited, and before explaining how a Bristol entrepreneur capitalised on the new technology, let us consider an early example of redundancy caused by the new service. Prior to 1852 it was the practice of Bristol merchants to wait in the Commercial Rooms for news of the safe return of their ships – there was even a weather vane and wind gauge readable from within the comfortable main room. Because it was always financially important to get notice of the impending arrival of their cargoes, there was an age-old system whereby, as soon as a returning ship moored in the King Road at the mouth of the River Avon, messengers known as 'pill warners' were dispatched on horseback to inform the anxiously waiting merchants that their goods had (hopefully) arrived safely. This enabled the forewarned merchant to start trading at the most advantageous price, and for this service the messengers were paid one guinea. The name pill warner originated from the village Crockerne Pill on the southern bank of the Avon opposite Shirehampton, which was the home of these messengers and of the river and Channel pilots. However, when the telegraph system arrived at the Commercial Rooms, the merchants arranged for a line to be laid to an office in Shirehampton for which they paid £30 per annum. After this, as well as doing away with many of the warners' jobs, for those pill warners who were still employed the rate was reduced to 2s 6d per message, a wage reduction of more than 88 per cent. The new telegraph message system also introduced the possibility of more dubious business opportunities before Bristol switched to GMT in September 1852. For example, a message dispatched over the telegraph wires from London, and time-stamped in London at twelve noon, would arrived in Bristol ten minutes and twenty-three seconds before noon.

**The Electrical Telegraph: A Bristolian Sees a Business Opportunity**
Sir George Biddell Airey, the 7th Astronomer Royal, instigated a telegraphic time service from Greenwich. The key to this service was a series of electrical impulses sent at agreed times of the day from the Royal Observatory at Greenwich, via Lothbury in London, to all those parts of the country connected to the new telegraph lines. The time impulse was used to ensure that all the railway and head Post Office clocks were synchronised with Greenwich. Shortly after the telegraph

system came to Bristol a proper telegram office was set up for general use on Broad Quay and the temporary office in the Commercial Rooms closed, although the members of the Rooms still had their own telegraphic link to Shirehampton. Records indicate that the new office was situated in the premises of Prices Nautical Instrument Maker next to the drawbridge on the quay. But it was one of their business neighbours and competitors a bit further along Broad Quay who saw the business potential in the time service, until then only used by the railways and the Post Office.

The person with the vision was William Langford of the Langford family firm of clockmakers. It was probably the awareness that a business competitor had a new technology almost within its grasp that spurred Langford into taking the iniative by negotiating with the Post Office for a rented 'time line' of his own. In 1852 he was able to agree a rate based upon the distance of his own premises from the main Post Office in Small Street, which was set at £17 per quarter. In his premises he installed an electrical indicator, called a galvanometer, which was connected to Greenwich 115 miles away via the special telegraph line, known as a chronopher. To make use of the system their senior clockmaker, at the appointed hour (for Langford this was at 10 o'clock), would stand by the galvanometer with a stopwatch. When the needle of the galvanometer gave a momentary deflection it signified that an electrical pulse had been received from Greenwich marking the agreed time to within a fraction of a second. This meant that Langford's could be certain that all their clocks could show GMT to within a fraction of a second a day – a hitherto unavailable accuracy for all but the best and most expensive regulator clocks.

The next thing that Langford did with this information is really the clever part. He sold the correct London time to leading members of Bristol's business and ecclesiastical communities. His customers included the cathedral, St Stephen's, the Commercial Rooms, the tobacco factories of W.D. & H.O. Wills at Redcliffe Street and Bedminster (as well as to their competitors, the British and American Tobacco Company at Ashton Gate), grain merchants Chamberlain, Pole & Co. in Union Street, the Bristol Tramways and Carriage Company – a total of at least nineteen of the main business organisations across the city. He did this by making use of another piece of what was then modern technology, a master-slave clock system, to synchronise the dials of other slave clocks.

The time signal galvanometer.

(A later slave-clock system was the 'Pul-Syn-Etic' developed by Alfred Ball in the 1920s.) Langford established direct-wire connections with each of his customers' premises, which enabled him to directly control their main clocks. His main customers, such as the W.D. & H.O. Wills factories, the Bristol Tramways and Carriage Company and the British and American Tobacco Company then used further slave-clock systems within their factories to control both timekeeping and office wall clocks.

**For Sale: 46 Million Minutes**

Although the direct-wire signal from Greenwich was discontinued in 1924 (more of that later), the Langford's direct-wire system to their customers continued until the Second World War blitz of 15 November 1941 destroyed their connecting cables across the city. By then the system had been superseded by newer technologies, such as the time pips, and it was decided not to reinstate the old system. But it still says much for William Langford's vision and quick thinking that he was able to buy eighty-nine years worth of time – a business monopoly that by any business criteria is an amazing record. During the century the Langford brothers' traditional clockmaking business also prospered and they entered into business alliances with their potential competitors, naming the new business at College Green, The Bristol Goldsmiths Alliance, for which they held a Royal Warrant and where they continued in business until the last of the brothers retired in 1964. Following this the business was run for a short while by a London firm before being closed and reopened as a music shop. Apart from a sadly defunct clock above the outside of the shop that still proclaims in faded gilt lettering 'Langford's Electric', there is still another sign of those heady days that remains. Set in the pavement directly below the clock is a small brass plate marking the Langford clock's distance in time from the Greenwich meridian. This plaque was donated on 26 June 1994 by Temple Local History Group to mark the centenary of the international acceptance of Greenwich as the prime meridian. The international centenary was also marked by a set of Royal Mail commemorative stamps.

**A 500-Year Curfew**
While still on matters horological let us consider the Church of St Nicholas at the corner of Baldwin Street, High Street and Bristol Bridge. A church dedicated to St Nicholas has been on this site for

Pavement plaque commemorating Langford family's enterprise.

more than 500 years, although the tower and part of the nave of the earliest one, similar to St John's Church at the bottom of Broad Street, sat over a gateway in the city wall. The line of the wall can still be traced on the ground by going along St Nicholas Street, crossing Corn Street, and continuing along Leonard, Bell and Tower Lanes and the Pithay, returning to the top of the High Street to complete the circuit. The early church was rebuilt in 1503 and again in 1762, and although the later one was almost destroyed in the blitz it has since been restored and today still provides an unusual time service, together with an even more unusual claim to fame.

One tradition that dates from 1481 and survives today is the nightly ringing of a curfew bell. This has nothing to do with Anti-Social Behaviour Orders – although, on reflection, it did in a way. The fifteenth-century curfew dates from the time when, except for the Norman Castle and the homes of wealthy merchants such as William Canynge, all buildings were made of wood and the threat of fire was a constant worry. The 9 p.m. curfew was imposed to ensure that after that time all fires were doused and no one should be on the streets carrying a light or a weapon, hence the ASBO aspect of the edict. The curfew (from the French for *couvre feu* meaning 'cover fire') was marked by the ringing of a tenor bell for fifteen minutes every night in St Nicholas Church. The bell was destroyed in the blitz, but by popular request was replaced as part of the restoration process and the tradition continued, still at 9 p.m., although nowadays it is only rung for seven-and-a-half minutes.

### If the Vestry Won't Pay Then the Devil Will

It seems from the Sheriff's records that there has been a clock in the tower of St Nicholas since at least 1517 and, as would be expected, 500 years of records itemise a variety of payments for repairs, replacements and enhancements. However, one enhancement that made the newspapers was associated with a replacement clock made by a London clockmaker, Mr Paine, in 1829. A novel design feature of Mr Paine's public clocks, which he had presented as a paper to the Royal Society a couple of years before and had installed in London and other towns, was a method for the automatic illumination of the clock dial. This was achieved by having the spaces between the numerals of the large skeleton iron dial filled with coloured glass. Gas lamps behind the dial were automatically ignited by a mechanism that derived its timing from the main clock. Bristol's brilliant new clock, announced in the *Bristol Gazette* on 19 March 1829, was easily visible to travellers approaching the city across Bristol Bridge from the south. The newspaper correspondent extolled its praises, but there turned out to be a fly in the ointment. A dispute over the cost arose between the gas company and the church Vestry who balked at the gas company's bill, with the result that the gas supply was cut off. After a week with a nice new non-illuminated clock, a satirical account of the dispute appeared in verse in a local newspaper, the last lines suggesting that, 'If the Vestry wouldn't pay then the Devil would'. Apparently stung by this public rebuke, the Vestry agreed to pay the gas bill and Mr Paine's dial was restored to its multicoloured splendour.

## George Edwin Lends a Hand

By the 1870s the clock of St Nicholas was due another makeover – not because there was anything fundamentally wrong with Mr Paine's clock, but because in the intervening years there had been a significant improvement in horological technology. This improvement was one of the new forms of escapement devised by Edmund Beckett Denison. A lawyer by profession, he developed an interest in tower clocks and became such a specialist on the subject that he was elected President of the British Horological Institute. Today he is more generally known by the title he took on being made a baronet, that of the first Lord Grimthorpe, and for the fact that he designed the clock at the Palace of Westminster, usually mistakenly called Big Ben, which in fact only refers to the bell. In horological circles he is probably best known for his invention of the double three-legged gravity escapement, the purpose of which was to disconnect any fluctuations caused by irregularities in the beat of the pendulum from the clock mechanism. Another of his beliefs, achievable in tower clocks, was that the pendulum should be as large and stiff as possible.

It would seem that another member of the Langford dynasty, George Edwin, was a disciple of Lord Grimthorpe's and used the opportunity of the makeover of St Nicholas' clock to incorporate the latter's new ideas. He also, as we can still see today, introduced a startling innovation of his own. Apart from making changes to the clock recommended by Lord Grimthorpe, in 1879 Edwin decided to add a dial to the south face of the clock. The extra dial was two-and-a-half feet in diameter and inset into the main seven-foot dial with a sweep-second hand (a long hand that measures seconds by moving the space of a minute for each second). According to the late Reginald Gibbs, the Langfords' senior clockmaker, there was a gentle technological rivalry within the family firm and Edwin believed that, with Lord Grimthorpe's theories and his own practical experience, he could make the St Nicholas clock intrinsically more accurate through good mechanical design than any new fangled electrical clocks that relied upon signals from London. Edwin added the sweep-second hand because he could – as he said, 'My own pocket watch has a second hand, so why shouldn't a public clock' – and because it provided a fine advertisement for the family firm.

So he achieved his objective with bells on – literally and figuratively! When the improvements were incorporated the new clock was able to keep time to within one second per week. A visitor to Bristol forty-six years later noted that it was still accurate to within one-and-a-half seconds. Edwin would have been justifiably proud of this achievement.

**What a Visitor to Bristol Most Wanted to See**
In the *Horological Journal* for April 1926 there is a report by John James Hall, a Fellow of the Royal Astronomical Society who, when met by his host at Temple Meads Railway Station, was asked if there was anything that he would particularly like to see during his visit. Back came the quick and unexpected reply: 'Yes, the great pendulum of St Nicholas.' The reason for this was that by 1926 it was known throughout scientific and engineering circles that as part of George Edwin's improvements, the pendulum of the St Nicholas clock was the longest in the country (22 feet 10.5 inches), and hence had the slowest beat at 2.5 seconds. It weighed a massive 1,350 pounds and the clock was so accurate that it could be adjusted to within one second a week by the addition or subtraction of a weight of 0.7 ounces onto the escapement mechanism. John James Hall was so impressed with Edwin's clock that he made a further two visits just to draw, photograph and note all the details. Today we should be thankful for his diligence because, although it was destroyed in the bombing of the church during the blitz, a full record nevertheless exists of this remarkable engineering achievement.

**Meet You Under the Tramways Clock**

Another of the Langford family achievements was the design of the 'geometric dial' for public clocks. They claimed, justifiably, that it 'heralded a new clarity and ease of reading the time on public clocks'. The firm never missed a publicity opportunity and this particular one arose when they were able to install the main clock for the Bristol Industrial & Fine Art Exhibition of 1893. This was probably a major achievement for Langfords and was, as far as we can tell, the first electric public clock in Bristol. According to their advertisement, Langford's geometric dial was designed to provide such a clarity of reading that, under normal circumstances, one was able to 'determine the time to a fraction of a minute'. Interestingly, although public clocks with analogue dials have since rather gone out of fashion, many being replaced by digital displays, the analogue dial clock can generally be read from a far greater distance than any digital display, illuminated or otherwise. Of course, now that everyone carries some sort of electronic wizardry with a built-in time display, public clocks aren't so important.

The site of the exhibition was on 'the Centre' in Colston Avenue, and is still marked today by a small fountain next to the Colston statue. This public drinking fountain was erected by the trustees using funds raised at the exhibition. Thanks to the success of their geometric dial it is easy to identify public clocks around the city that were either designed or modified by the Langfords. The most recognisable of these, and the most quoted, is the Tramways Clock. The three-dial square-boxed clock is over the pavement on the Centre, outside what used to be the head office of the Bristol Tramways and Carriage Company. Although the firm has long gone, it is still known as the Tramways Clock, and probably because of its large and clear geometric dial it has become a city landmark and famous trysting place. I wonder how many Bristolians' very existence started with the statement, 'Meet you under the Tramways Clock'?

**Getting to Work on Time**

Modern timekeeping systems have made the 'works clock' redundant. This, together with changed work practices and the closing of most of the factories that were once Langford's customers, has meant that many of these masterpieces, made by the clockmaker's skill, have ended up in scrap yards. One Bristol company that was probably best known as the maker of all 1950s schoolboys' essential swap kits, was the packaging and printing firm of Mardon, Son & Hall, which was also responsible for researching and making cigarette cards (stiffeners) for W.D. & H.O. Wills. One day Mrs Joyce Williams, who once worked in the Chemistry Research Department of Mardon's No. 14 Factory, which used to be in Redcliffe Street, spotted a forlorn relic of her former workplace lying in the humiliating surroundings of a Hartcliffe scrap yard. Understandably upset by her discovery, she wrote this poem, which she has kindly allowed me to reproduce here. It was first published in their company house journal, *The Caxtonian*. The subject of her poem was the main clock from the front of the factory, which would have been all too familiar to Mardonians hurrying to 'clock on' in time and makes a fitting epitaph for all the clocks and timekeeping systems discussed in this chapter. She begins the poem with the lines:

> Stands the firm's clock at 25 to 9?
> And draw they still the crimson line?

Joyce's 'crimson line' dates back to the days when office staff, even if they didn't punch a time-clock card, still had to sign in the office register stating their arrival time. At 25 to 9 a red line was drawn across the page and anyone arriving 'below that line' was late and was dealt with accordingly. Ironically nowadays many office employees would consider the practice an 'infringement upon their liberty', whilst still accepting that opting to take a lunch break could be a career-limiting decision! A case of *plus ça change, plus c'est la même chose*?

> Here in a dealer's desert yard
> Among the lumber cast away
> And relics ruthless years discard
> Is time itself in time's decay.
> No more to draw the office bound
> The early, late, the fleet or slow
> And whirl them on its daily round
> And bid them come or stay or go.
> The hours it tallied numberless

Are swept away as leaves that fall
And days advance and months progress
And years decline – and this is all.

Time needs no engine to record
How fickle modes corrupt and rust,
But with a grim pathetic hoard
Itself redundant gathers dust.

**Footnote**

To end on a more cheerful note, here is another Bristol curiosity in the form of a riddle. Where is it possible to see a four-footed clock with six hands, and three faces?

The answer can be found on the Broad Street frontage of Christ Church. At this spot, the carfax – where the four main streets (Broad Street, Corn Street, Wine Street and High Street) of the medieval city meet – a clock is flanked by two Quarter Jacks, life-size automata that strike the bells on the quarter hours. Hence, two hands and one face on the clock…the rest you have, no doubt already worked out for yourself.

# 10

# WHERE ARE THE DOVES?
# THE LIVES AND TIMES OF THE TEMPLARS
# IN BRISTOL

## A Bristol Landmark

One of Bristol's famous landmarks that can be seen from Victoria Street is the leaning tower of the fourteenth-century Temple Church. But how many Bristolians realise that within the church's burnt-out

Temple Church tower.

shell (from the blitz), the outlines of a much earlier round church that was built by the Knights Templar can still be seen? But why here, as everyone knows that the crusaders were based in the Holy Land, not in downtown Bristol? The reason Bristol was the home of not one, but two crusader churches is because the land southeast of Bristol Bridge, between Victoria Street and the river towards Temple Meads, was once the estate of two orders of crusader knights.

Nowadays there are very few visible clues to its eventful past, although they can still be found if you know where to look. Mention of crusaders conjures up a picture of mounted knights fighting the Saracens for possession of the Holy Land, or protecting pilgrims on their way to Jerusalem, but what has this got to do with Bristol?

### A New Crusading Order

The Christian capture of Jerusalem by the first crusade in 1099 allowed pilgrims from Western Europe to travel to the Holy Land, but the way was long and perilous and many fell by the wayside before ever reaching the holy city. To remedy the situation a small group of French knights were invited to establish a presence in Jerusalem as well as organising safe passage for pilgrims. However, it was ten years before they were given official recognition by the Council of Troyes. Their sponsorship at Troyes by Count Fulk of Anjou and Bernard, Abbot of Clairvaux, resulted in their being granted the status in 1118 of a monastic order, to be known henceforth as the Poor Knights of the Temple of Solomon of Jerusalem, generally shortened to 'The Templars'. This was a monastic order with the usual vows of poverty and chastity, but with a startling new development: the 'knights' were allowed to bear arms. As an order of 'soldier monks' they were still governed by a master and a set of monastic rules, but wore a white robe as a symbol of purity, emblazoned with a red cross, which served to remind them of their oath to be ready to shed their blood in the defence of Christendom. Although guarding pilgrims to the Holy Land is the recorded reason for their formation, much has been made of unrecorded activities of the small group of founding knights while they were in Jerusalem for almost a decade before they were officially recognised. In recent years they have been the subject of many con-spiracy theories usually involving buried treasure, improbable lineages and privileged access to arcane knowledge. A cynic might comment on an apparent causal relationship between some of the more outré theories and publishers' cash.

To find out why the Templars were in England we need to look at how their order grew from a group of nine knights empowered to guard pilgrims en route to Jerusalem to becoming the richest and most powerful of the monastic orders. When the pilgrim route was made safer by the Templars' presence, a pilgrimage to Jerusalem and the Holy Land was made possible for many more people who saw it as both a Christian ideal and, often, as a way of completing a penance. As a papal monastic order, the Templars quickly attracted donations and gifts of land, often from pious landowners who were encouraged by the Church to offer gifts or endowments as an acceptable alternative to undertaking a pilgrimage themselves.

## Crusaders Come to Bristol

Bristol's first recorded involvement with the crusaders began in 1145 when Robert De Berkeley granted them enough land on part of his manor of Bedminster, in the bend of the Avon just south of Bristol, to establish a small community. Records show that this initially comprised a small church, a communal hall and twenty-eight dwellings and other buildings. Modern-day evidence of the Templars' occupation is mostly limited to the results of archaeological investigation and place names. However, it is still possible to trace the outline of the

Preserved outline of the Templars' round church, Bristol.

Templars' twelfth-century church as it is marked out in gravel inside the bombed ruins of the later fourteenth-century Temple Church, which is now under the custodianship of English Heritage. The reason for the Templars' round churches is that they were inspired by the Church of the Holy Sepulchre in Jerusalem, and in England other examples can be seen in London, Cambridge, Garway in Herefordshire, and at Little Maplestead in Essex.

## Bristol's Role

Although the order grew rich through benefactions it still needed substantial earned income to support its rapidly growing organisation and the infrastructure necessary to guard the long pilgrimage routes. The value of establishments (known as preceptories), such as that at Bristol was that they provided the order with a day-to-day income through agriculture and related trading activities. However, in the case of Bristol it is more likely that the site was chosen initially for its logistic location rather than for cash crops, especially as the land they had been given bordered a bend in the River Avon. The ground was soft and marshy, hence the spectacular lean of the tower of Temple Church. In an attempt to correct the tower's lean, the second stage was built at a different angle, which explains why, as well as leaning, it has a kink halfway up.

Looking at the centres of crusader influence mapped across the wool production areas of the West Country it is possible to see that the knights had a presence in an area from just below Gloucester, across to Wootton Bassett, Salisbury, Bradford-on-Avon, Bruton, Shepton Mallet, Tiverton, Wells, Bristol, the Vale of Severn and back to Gloucester, thus putting Bristol in a key location to act as a port for the shipment of wool and other commodities.

Although the Templars' presence has always been known, the first direct evidence for its logistic importance came about during the 1980s as a result of research carried out by the Temple Local History Group. They were recording the history of what is now known as Temple parish when they noticed that a 1673 map drawn by Jacobus Millerd, although long after the Templar era, still showed a small inlet or creek at the end of the present-day Water Lane. Further searches showed that the artist F.G. Lewin RWA had also included it in one of his 1920s panoramic sketches of the area, but complete with a small

Temple Fee, as it may have looked in 1200.

ship moored at a dock in the inlet. At that time it was not possible to find any justification for these interpretations of the landscape, and the generally held opinion was that it was probably just artistic licence, Lewin having probably taken his lead from Millerd's map. There the research might have ended if it hadn't been for a discovery made by Michael Baigent who, whilst carrying out his own research in the La Rochelle port rolls, came across the names of two of the Templars' own ships, named *La Templere* and *Le Buscard*, both registered at Bristol. As a result of this discovery a more detailed search for evidence of a creek or dock was undertaken. However, the key piece of evidence arose from a chance conversation with Joseph Bryant who was researching his family's rope-making business at the adjacent Temple Back (the road that now runs alongside the river). He was able to confirm from a deed in his family's possession that an ancestor had granted a 99-year lease to a carpenter, Samuel Whiting, on the land adjacent to the River Avon at Temple Back, subject to him 'building a new dwelling' (rope-making house) and, 'Arch over the dock at the east end of Water Lane', effectively culverting the dock that was shown on the early map. The date of the deed tied in with Millerd's map. Armed with this information, more research was carried out, which led to the discovery of further corroboratory evidence.

So we know that Templars had a base in Bristol with their own estate or preceptory complete with church, houses, a hall, a dock, and their own ships. Although records of other buildings haven't yet been found, it is likely they would also have had warehouse space for the goods, unless they used part of the hall, and lodgings would also have been needed for the ships' crews, being so close to the port of Bristol.

Based on records of other Templar preceptories it seems the Templars' Hall would have been the main communal building where they met and ate their meals. It would have been a busy place because at any one time, there could have been about thirty men entitled to eat there – typically five brothers, a few pensioners, half a dozen at the esquires' table, plus tenant labourers or even Templar sailors. The smaller preceptories, such as this one at Bristol, far from the fighting overseas, would typically have been in the control of a single knight, often a retired crusader.

As well as river and dock access they would have also needed road access and the earliest records we have for Temple Street are 1242. This is known because of a tragic accident that made legal history. Early Bristol charters tell of a boy who was killed in Temple Street by a pillory that fell on him. It seems that two of the Templars' horses had been tethered to it and something caused them to bolt, pulling over the pillory. In accordance with the law of the land, whenever an inanimate object caused a death, a fine, known as a Deodand, based upon the valuation of the object, was payable for the life of the departed. In this instance the Deodand was assessed as ten shillings for the horses and two shillings for the pillory. This was to appease the wrath of God. However, in this instance a problem arose because the Templars as a monastic order did not recognise any local authority and claimed that they were only answerable to papal authority, which overruled any other. As such, they refused to appear before the local justices. The issue was finally resolved by their agreeing to make an *ex gratia* payment of twelve shillings to the Sheriff, an amount equivalent to the Deodand.

Another aspect of their autocracy that made them very unpopular was that they claimed exemption from all local tithes, bridge tolls and similar dues and were not answerable to the town for any of their actions. Although many of the books written about the history of Bristol have referred to the continued conflicts between the Burgesses of Bristol and the Templars, to date the legal issue over the Deodand is the only one found worthy of recording in the charters and, importantly, it gives an insight into their behaviour, as well as our earliest early recorded name for Temple Street. As if the issue of the boy who was killed wasn't enough, there was yet another reason for their unpopularity. The Templars' claim of legal immunity from the local authority also extended to their (non-Templar) tenants. So a situation could arise – and probably did – where their secular villeins could commit a civil offence north of Bristol Bridge in the town and flee back over the bridge to the sanctuary of Temple Fee. No wonder the Burgesses of Bristol appealed to the King to give them control over the inhabitants south of the Avon! This does not mean that the tenants would not have been punished by the Templars – remember the pillory that was located in Temple Street?

### The Final Days
These types of arguments and general bad feelings simmered away until the early fourteenth century when matters came to a head. By this time the Templar Order had become amazingly powerful (their financial acumen meant that they were even lending money to kings), but their downfall had begun in 1291 when the Mamelukes took control of the fortress of Acre, and the Templars had to abandon the Holy Land. This meant that the Templars' days were numbered. One notable and dangerous royal creditor was Philip IV of France, who put pressure on Pope Clement V to dissolve the order and confiscate all their wealth. The main arguments put to the Pope for their suppression were not that Philip owed them a lot of money (that was just a coincidence), but that the Templars had indulged in obscene and sacrilegious practices. Although the Pope tried to delay making a decision, the fact that he was a virtual captive at Avignon in France made resisting Philip's demands very difficult, and eventually in 1307 the Pope acquiesced and signed a secret order for the simultaneous apprehension of all Templars, wherever they were. Thus the age of the Knights Templars, which had lasted from 1118 until 1307, came to an end. Many of the Templar lands and buildings were subsequently taken over by the older but surviving order of the Hospital of St John of Jerusalem, the Knights Hospitaller (the builders of Bristol's landmark leaning tower).

### The Templars' Successors at Bristol
Some of the books written about the dissolution of the order give the impression that upon the dissolution, which dragged on until 1312, the estates and property of the Templars were then just handed over to the Knights Hospitaller. However, this is a misconception, as in some instances properties were not transferred until the 1330s, by which

time many of the Templar estates, such as the one at Bristol, had been plundered by the Crown.

What happened to all the Templars' wealth? Is it buried somewhere in Bristol? This is highly unlikely because after the dissolution and arrest of the Templars in 1307 an inventory of all their estates was carried out, but by the time this was completed it is not surprising that many of the remaining preceptories were in a state of decline. Following the arrests, the preceptories were leaderless (more about that later) and their houses were unmaintained. The situation was made worse because after the final dissolution in 1312, any surviving brothers were sent away by the Church to serve penances at other monastic houses around the country to gain absolution from their alleged sins.

**Grand Larceny**
In England, although Edward II showed an initial reluctance to enforce the arrest of the Templars, his situation was similar to that of Philip of France – he had no money. In Edward's case it had been squandered on ill-conceived campaigns, buying loyalty, and on gifts for his favourites. However, he soon realised that the Pope's call for the dissolution of the order gave him a solution to many of his financial problems – in other words the Papal Bull of 13 March 1312 gave him a licence to plunder the Templar estates to clear his debts. For example, once the leading Templars were locked up and the brethren dispersed, the King took £360 worth of Templar fleeces and had them shipped to one of his Italian creditors as part payment of a debt. He also used their funds and any remaining produce or assets from their estates to pay bills still outstanding from his Scottish campaigns, such as Bannockburn. However, much of the Templars' wealth in England was used to buy the loyalty of feudal barons and reward favourites, Piers Galveston being the most infamous. As an example of the sums involved, the Scottish campaign took £464, nearly double the total amount of the annual returns of all the Warwickshire Templar manors. Much of the Templars' wealth came from bequests such as the gift of the Bristol estate by Robert De Berkeley, but probably not an inconsiderable amount also came from tenants' estates.

As outlined above, the Templars were unpopular with towns such as Bristol because they consistently rode roughshod over local rules and flouted town ordinances, but they were also not too popular with their tenants. It is not generally realised that the Templars as landlords included a very unpopular clause in their tenancy agreements. This clause was the 'Obit' or death duty. At that time the law of the land stated that after settling any debts the residue of a person's estate was divided as follows: one third to the wife, one third to the children, and the remaining third could be disposed of at will, unless the deceased had been a Templar tenant, in which case they were forced by Templar regulations to will the remaining third to their Templar Lord. (Nowadays of course this is called Inheritance Tax – perhaps a trick the Chancellor picked up from the Templars?)

## Petty Larceny

The King's officers were so keen to get the Templars behind bars that they neglected to put in place caretaker landlords before carting the Templars off to London's 'gate' jails. The absence of any caretakers, together with the Templars' unpopularity at the grass-roots level, probably explains why almost as soon as they were arrested their former villeins indulged in understandably opportunistic looting. One gets the image of the Templars being led away in chains, and before they and their captors had even vanished over the first hill, everything movable including spoons, salt cellars and keys were being carried out of the preceptory's back door! For example, by the time the King's inspectors arrived to take stock at one West Country Templar estate, it was noticed that the doves were missing from the dovecote. Other inventory 'shortcomings' included the full range of livestock and pro-visions, such as chickens, horses, cheese, butter, sides of bacon and beef, casks of cider and wine.

Although no mercy would have been shown to anyone caught with any of these items, to put the thefts in perspective, compare the above examples of petty larceny with the following list of Templar property appropriated by King Edward to support his Scottish campaign: 1,000 quarters of wheat, 1,000 quarters of oats, 200 quarters of peas and beans, 300 tuns of wine, 3 tuns of honey, 200 quarters of salt, 1,000 stockfish (salt cod); as well as large quantities of grain and livestock. Another trick the King used to clear his debts was to use plundered lands to pay off arrears of salary. He did this by making a grant of land to an official for his use and income until the amount owed for past service had been cleared. For example, in Bristol in 1318 Sir Richard

Amory passed to the Prior and Fraternity of St Augustine an acre of land next to what is now Temple Gate. It seems that he had been granted use of the land for the eight years. Until the dissolution this land would have been part of the Bristol Templar estate, and Sir Richard Amory's grant to the Augustinians possibly signified the end of his arrangement with the King.

In this way, including of course outright gifts to his favourites, about half the Templar property ended up with the King and his barons, and after many years the remainder, such as the balance of the Bristol estate, was eventually obtained by the Hospitallers who themselves lost it all at the Reformation. Ironically, although the Order of Hospitallers didn't survive the Reformation of Henry VIII, their church did. This was because both Temple Church and the Priory of St James, by the Horsefair, had become parish churches and were therefore allowed to continue. Thus Temple Church continued as a place of worship used, if not by the Templars or Knights of St John, at least by the residents of Temple parish until the church was gutted on the night of 24 November 1940 by incendiary bombs during a Second World War blitz. However, the church that survived the dissolution of the order, the Reformation, and almost survived Hitler's blitzkreig, nearly suffered a final indignity when army sappers thought that the lean (the 115-feet-high tower is 4 feet out of alignment) was due to bomb damage, and were only just prevented from pulling it down for safety reasons. All of this explains why today the only reminders in Bristol of the crusading Templars are names such as Temple Meads, the public house called Knights Templar and the landmark of the leaning church tower.

# 11

# BIZARRE BELIEFS AND ODD OCCURRENCES

Bizarre though some beliefs may be, nevertheless they are usually firmly held in spite of all evidence to the contrary. Here is a small selection of some of the zanier beliefs that have contributed towards the rich tapestry of life in Bristol.

## A Hundred Gallons of Frogs

There was a belief that consumption was caused by the ingestion of excessive amounts of green tea – a belief that led to Bristol's very own plague of frogs, scares of a French Jacobin plot, and a threatened outbreak of politically motivated arson. Even though green tea has been recommended as a health aid for many thousands of years and is currently very popular, it was also in vogue especially amongst the young ladies of Bristol during the early 1800s. However, not everybody was convinced of its medicinal powers – in fact quite the opposite. One leader of the medical fraternity was convinced that the drinking of excessive quantities of green tea by young ladies was a cause of pulmonary consumption or TB. The medical gentleman was the famous Dr Beddoes, described by a contemporary as 'uncommonly short and fat, with little elegance of manners, and nothing characteristic externally of genius or science; extremely silent, and, in a few words, a very bad companion'. Although apparently cold mannered, when Beddoes was involved in conversation he had a wild and active imagination and his personality was sufficient to act as a magnet to the intellects of the day. His home at Rodney Place in Clifton was a rallying point for Coleridge, Wedgwood, Roget (who had a word for it), and Southey, not forgetting of course, his most famous protégé Humphry Davy, whom he appointed Superintendent of his Pneumatic Institute in Dowry Square, Hotwells, in October 1798. The appointment was a significant career step for young Davy, newly arrived from his home town of Penzance. Two of Davy's most famous discoveries were 'laughing gas', the world's first anaesthetic gas nitrous oxide, and the principles of gas combustion that led to the

Memorial at Rodney Place, Clifton, to Thomas Beddoes MD, his family and his protégé.

invention of the miners' safety lamp, an invention that must have saved tens of thousands of lives.

It was this intellectual environment and Dr Beddoes' preoccupation with the scourge of the age, tuberculosis – or consumption as it was then known– that led to some unusual experiments. One much-recorded idea was his proposal that consumptives should share their bedroom with a dairy cow. As a biographer said, this was an example of Beddoes' 'rational eccentricity'. The reason for the presence of a cow, was not to breathe all over the patients, or moo them to sleep, but rather to provide a constant temperature, which in nineteenth-century houses was basically impossible.

But let us return to Dr Beddoes' concerns about green tea. He planned to carry out an experiment to prove that green tea in large quantities was injurious to health. In order to demonstrate this he had arranged for two equal-sized ponds to be dug, one was to be filled with fresh water and the other with green tea. Into these ponds he proposed to release a quantity of frogs and he made arrangements with a friend in

Shropshire to capture a sufficient number for his experiment and ship them to Bristol. In due course a hogshead full of frogs arrived at Bristol Docks (a hogshead cask could contain between 63 and 140 gallons).

Unfortunately, while unloading them from the ship, the rope on the crane broke, dropping the hogshead onto the quay and causing it to break asunder releasing, it is said, 10,000 frogs – much to the frogs' joy. Many hopped into the River Frome, much to the alarm of the local citizens who must have thought they had been transported back in time to Biblical Egypt. At this point the situation got nasty. This was a God-fearing age and most people knew their bible stories, in this case, Exodus 8:2, 'I will smite all thy borders with Frogs' and, Exodus 8:7, 'magicians brought up frogs on the land'. Whether it was the wording of these verses that alarmed and upset the people, or similar passages from the Psalms or the Book of Revelations, we will never know. However, we do know that because of the political climate the word was quickly spread around that the doctor was really a traitor who was harbouring French Jacobins in his cellar. They believed that the frogs, hidden in a barrel, were to be secretly delivered to his house where they had been intended as sustenance for his cellar full of foreign insurgents. Some people even spoke of burning his house down and a crowd made their way to Dr Beddoes' home at Rodney Place. Fortunately for the doctor and his neighbours they was met by someone able to calm them and dissuade them from their arsonistic intents. The calming influence that saved the day was a fellow doctor, who explained to them that the frogs were intended for dissection and use in Humphry Davy's galvanic experiments.

It likely that the number of frogs that fell onto the quayside was closer to 300 than 10,000. As for the frogs, most of those which fell into the nineteenth-century open sewer that was at that time the River Frome quickly died, while those that were gathered up from the quayside and saved for the good doctor were sacrificed in the cause of science. The account of this amphibian mêlée, recounted in *Felix Farley's Journal* for 24 September and 1 October 1836 never explained what use was made of the pond full of green tea. Perhaps they held a soirée for the young ladies of Clifton? So next time you see a green frog in a Bristol pond, remember to ask it, 'My dear, are you a surviving descendant of the well known Shropshire frogs? I only ask because you do have a distinctly green tinge.'

## Bristol's Secret Police Force

Edwardian prosperity saw a significant expansion of the suburbs with shopkeepers and traders being able to afford larger houses away from their place of work in the city. In particular, two of these new housing estates were the New Clifton estate near Coldharbour Road and the Edwards estate along the new road that ran alongside the Cran Brook. It was activities associated with one of these houses in Cranbrook Road that gave rise to a particularly bizarre belief.

For many years there was a house that no one was ever seen entering or leaving. The windows were cleaned, the grass was regularly and mysteriously cut, but there was never any sign of any occupants or even rubbish bins put out for collection. People's curiosity about this mystery house grew, until one day some of the original residents gave the following explanation.

In the 1920s they and others moved from the centre of Bristol to this new estate that seemed so far out of Bristol that their friends were concerned that they wouldn't ever be able to visit. They were also concerned about the Gypsy encampment on the banks of the Cran directly behind

### Buses—continued.

## New Clifton, Zetland Road and Tramways Centre.

Buses run every 12 minutes Week-days & Sundays

| SERVICE No. 19. | | WEEK-DAYS | | SUNDAYS | |
|---|---|---|---|---|---|
| | | First am | Last pm | First pm | Last pm |
| North View | dep, | 8 0 | 11 0 | 2 12 | 10 0 |
| Clare Avenue | ,, | 8 4 | 11 4 | 2 16 | 10 4 |
| Zetland Road | ,, | 8 7 | 11 7 | 2 20 | 10 7 |
| Top Stokes Croft | ,, | 8 10 | 11 10 | 2 22 | 10 10 |
| Royal Infirmary | ,, | 8 14 | 11 14 | 2 26 | 10 14 |
| Tramways Centre | arr. | 8 17 | 11 17 | 2 30 | 10 17 |
| | | First am | Last pm | First pm | Last pm |
| Tramways Centre | dep. | 8 24 | 11 24 | 2 36 | 10 24 |
| Royal Infirmary | ,, | 8 28 | 11 28 | 2 40 | 10 28 |
| Top Stokes Croft | ,, | 8 32 | 11 32 | 2 44 | 10 31 |
| Zetland Road | ,, | 8 34 | 11 34 | 2 46 | 10 34 |
| Clare Avenue | ,, | 8 38 | 11 38 | 2 50 | 10 38 |
| North View | arr. | 8 42 | 11 42 | 2 54 | 10 41 |

FARES. Tramways Centre and Zetland Road, 1d.; Top Stokes Croft and Clare Avenue, 1d.; Zetland Road Junction and North View. 1d.; All the way, 2d.

A bus timetable for service No.19 on the new Clifton estate, November 1914.

their house, and if there was trouble, where would a policeman be if they needed one? However, all these fears were allayed when it was explained to them that the apparently empty house was not really a house at all. When the new housing estate was laid out, the civic authorities made special arrangements for the policing of the area, the nearest police stations being in Redland and Somerville Road. The special arrangements, so these people believed, were that the authorities had a tunnel dug all the way from the Redland Road police station to the empty house in Cranbrook Road, and that the 'house' was just a disguised tunnel exit, so that in the event of any 'civil insurrection' police reinforcements could be rushed through the tunnel, presumably with truncheons at the ready. This has always conjured up a mental image of a long file of silver-buttoned Bobbies, with truncheons at the ready, just like a scene from Gilbert and Sullivan's operetta, *Pirates of Penzance*, jogging through the tunnel whilst singing jolly policemen's songs such as 'When a Felon's Not Engaged in his Employment', obviously with special emphasis on the line 'He loves to hear the little brook a gurgling' or the chorus 'With cat-like tread'.

Intrigued by the persistence of this very local belief, in spite of its apparent absurdity, further enquiries revealed a possible explanation. The stream, the Cran brook, rises from springs in Redland Green and, combining with other small springs, runs through the valley between the allotments and Redland Green Farm into Dugar Walk where it was culverted, when the house building extended down the hill. The stream flows underground down Cranbrook Road, across and beneath Clare Avenue, continuing underground in the culvert or tunnel until it briefly emerges further down flowing between the houses in Cranbrook and Elton Road. The stream originally crossed beneath Cheltenham Road and continued down to feed Rennison's Baths, eventually ending up as a small creek on the north bank of the River Frome. Credulous new residents coming from the 'city', having perhaps enquired about the reason for the building of a tunnel beneath Dugar Walk and Cranbrook Road, seemingly from the direction of Redland police station, were kidded into believing the story.

There is a simple but sad explanation for the mysteriously empty house. The owner had been taken into long-term care, and the house was administered by the Court of Protection, and couldn't be sold, just maintained, and thus it was for many decades. Sorry to spoil an interesting urban myth.

## The Strange Case of the Painter's Head

It was a Thursday night on 16 January 1777 when a man, known as Peter the Painter, walked quietly along the quayside searching for three particular ships amongst the many crowding the quays. At last he found them. The first one was the *Savannah la Mar* being loaded for Jamaica, and his luck was in, the other two ships he sought, the privateer *Fame* and the ship *Hibernia*, were also at nearby berths. He had chosen his moment well; a low tide, which meant that the ships would be aground on the mud (it would be another quarter of a century before the floating harbour was constructed), and an overcast sky gave him easy access without attracting the attention of the watch. He quickly went from ship to ship placing the materials he had gathered, together with his own design of a delayed-action incendiary, before setting light to it and making off. To his annoyance his devices were spotted and extinguished before they had a chance to cause serious damage to the ships. He then made his way to the warehouse of James Morgan, the Corn Street druggist, and attempted to start a fire there, but again the fire was spotted before much damage was done. Undeterred by his failures, at the weekend he struck again. This time he was successful and managed to set fire to three warehouses in Bell Lane, and before the fires could be extinguished a total of six buildings were destroyed.

Apart from the considerable damage he managed to cause, Peter the Painter was probably pleased that his actions also provoked a row between the local political parties, who blamed each other's supporters for his arson, which they correctly assumed had been aimed at anti-American businesses and merchants. However, the saboteur's pleasure was short-lived because the outrage his actions caused resulted in rewards being offered for his capture. After his arson in Bristol he headed on foot to London, thieving and housebreaking along the way in order to feed himself. By this time people had managed to circulate broadsheets describing him as 5 feet 7 inches in height, with sandy hair, a pale and freckled complexion, wearing a rumpled brown coat. This description encouraged Bristol merchants to put up 500 guineas with the King adding £1,000 and the MP Edmund Burke a further £50. The reason for the relatively large reward was that in the meantime other intelligence had been received that these arson attacks were likely to be the work of the same arsonist or group who had tried to fire the strategically important rope house in Portsmouth dockyard.

Peter the Painter, as far as anyone can tell, was a Scotsman born in Edinburgh, whose real name was either James Aitkin or possibly James Hill. Whatever his real name, the broadsheet description was good enough for the Andover jail keeper and a local shopkeeper to remember seeing him pass through the town. The alarm was raised and some locals gave chase, 'Peter' was caught, taken in chains to the Assize at Winchester, found guilty of arson and taken back to Portsmouth. There he was executed on 10 March 1777 by being hung from a 65-foot mizzen mast specially erected by the Victory Gate. Interestingly, it was less than twenty years ago that the act that carried the death penalty for arson in the Royal Dockyards was repealed.

The way Peter's body was dealt with after his execution possibly explains how the following Bristol belief came into being. As was common practice, after his body was cut down it was put in a cage and hung in a prominent position in an effort to discourage any other saboteurs, as well as provide food for the crows and seagulls. Not surprisingly, over the course of time his body parts disappeared or were dispersed. It was this disappearance, coupled with a restoration in Bristol that gave rise to a rather strange belief.

When one of the destroyed warehouses in Quay Street was rebuilt, Mr Rosser the stonemason responsible for the rebuilding made use of stone and some corbels from the ruins of Keynsham Abbey. One of the corbels was of a man's head and the local belief, in spite of all evidence to the contrary, was that that this stone head was really the skull of Peter the Painter, the pro-American arsonist who had destroyed the warehouse. Unfortunately the 'skull' was lost in subsequent building redevelopments – so now we shall never know for certain.

## Bristol's Mythical Founders

The origins of Bristol are, as the cliché goes, 'shrouded in mystery', but as ever the void will always be filled by a good story, or in this case dozens of stories. Two statues, believed to represent Bristol's founders, are set in niches on either side of the last remaining gateway in the city's medieval wall, St John's Arch (named for the church of St John the Baptist built into the wall with the church spire sited directly above the gateway). The church dates from 1370 but Nicholls and Taylor writing in *Bristol Past and Present* in 1881 believed the statues had come from an earlier building.

Although it is generally accepted that there was a Saxon settlement on the site of Castle Park and a variety of Roman artefacts have been found from a number of sites across the city, there is nothing so far to suggest that Bristol existed as a Roman town or that they built on an earlier settlement at this location. The Romans' nearest known station, Abonae, was four miles away downriver at Sea Mills. There is archaeological evidence of early defensible settlements near Bristol on the Clifton Downs, with earthworks adjacent to the present-day Observatory Tower, and others on the opposite side of the River Avon at Stokeleigh and Burwalls. However, there is no firm evidence to prove that early Bristol was founded by ancient rulers, brothers called Brennus and Belinus – the supposed identity of the two statues flanking St John's gate at the bottom of Broad Street. In spite of lack of evidence or maybe because of it, medieval chroniclers who were in the habit of writing historical romances based upon spurious genealogies, set Bristol's origins as pre-Roman or even hundreds of years before Christ.

As a result of the fact that a number of these early romances quoted each other as sources, and the accounts are further complicated by the passage of time, it is impossible to say with any certainty which if any of the accounts are true. Nevertheless, Robert Ricart a fifteenth-century Town Clerk and historian believed the numerous accounts that ascribed the founding of Bristol to Bran, Bryn, Brynne or Brennus.

The names and exploits of Brennus and Belinus and their father Malmutius have been enshrined in English literature through references such as those in Shakespeare's *Cymbeline* and Edmund Spenser's *The Faerie Queene*. In *Cymbeline*, Act III, Scene I, set in a room of state in Cymbeline's palace in Britain we see King Cymbeline, the Queen, his stepson Cloten and Lords enter through one door and, through another door, Caius Lucius, Roman General and his attendants. Cymbeline pronounces:

> We do say then to Caesar,
> Our ancestor was that Mulmutius, which
> Ordained our laws; (whose use the sword of Caesar
> Hath too much mangled: whose repair, and franchise,
> Shall, by the power we hold, be our good deed,
> Though Rome be therefore angry); Mulmutius,

Who was the first of Britain, which did put
His brows within a golden crown, and call'd
Himself King.

Shakespeare's Mulmutius would have been Dyvnwal Moelmud,
latinised as *Dunwallo Malmutius*, who was reported to have reigned
about 500 BCE, firstly over Cornwall, then over the whole of Britain.
When he died, his sons Brennus and Belinus reigned jointly over
Britain. Steevens, the Shakespearean scholar writing in 1823, said that
he believed that although Shakespeare is thought to have written
*Cymbeline* in about 1609 he was able to use incidents for the general
scheme of the play from Giovanni Boccaccio's *Decameron*, a printed
translation of which appeared in this country in 1620. Also, it is more
than likely that Shakespeare would have been familiar with the work of
Edmund Spenser (1552–99), who wrote in *The Faerie Queene* about
the battles and victories of Brennus and Belinus. He described them as:

Donwallo dyde (for what may liue for ay?)
And left two sonnes, of pearelesse prowesse both;
That sacked Rome too dearely did assay,
The recompence of their periured oth,
And ransackt Greece well tryde, whe[n] they were wroth;
Besides subiected Fraunce, and Germany,
Which yet their prayses speake, all be they loth,
And inly tremble at the memory
Of Brennus and Bellinus, kings of Britany.

Another person who supported the myth was John Corry, a prolific
author who flourished around 1825 and who included in his works a
number of town histories, including one of Bristol, published in 1810.
In his Bristol book he claimed that Brennus enlarged and improved
the town, which was already of some consequence, and contributed by
his royal patronage to the prosperity of Bristol. He cited the presence
of the statues on either side of the city gate as proof of his assertion.
His sources are unknown, although it is possible that he drew on these
aforementioned accounts and possibly others such as Geoffrey of
Monmouth, The Duke of Norfolk (Thomas Howard), and John
Leland. However, the sources used by Geoffrey for his work, the

*History of the Kings of Britain* are now recognised as questionable; the Duke of Norfolk was trying to prove a Tudor genealogy, and John Leland, although diligent, was foremost a chronicler and was willing to accept tales as told. What all these accounts have in common is that they indicate a general desire to believe that these early kings of Britain founded Bristol, which as conjecture is not unreasonable. However, it would be nice to have some concrete, rather than merely stone, evidence. Although in view of the lack of firm evidence it is reasonable to say that the belief is pure fiction, and that it has just been a case of each chronicler cribbing off his predecessor, we must also remember that Robert Ricart had access to the records of the nationally important Kalendaries, of which all but a few were swept away in a fire, and which would have predated most of these other accounts. Shakespeare is reported to have visited Bristol, leading one to wonder if he saw the statues, asked about them and as a result picked up on the tale that eventually he used for Cymbeline.

Nevertheless, while Nicholls and Taylor, the nineteenth-century historians researching Bristol's history, accepted that the story of Brennus and Belinus was firmly believed by Bristolians and that the story has indeed been written into most early histories, they could place no confidence in 'these vain traditions'.

As part of the 2006 programme of restoration of St John's Church and tower the two 'founders' statues were also restored, at which time the left-hand statue had its right forearm replaced (in an engraving by H.O. Neil in 1820 it was shown as missing), together with the addition of gilded crosses on the orbs that each hold in their left hand. The sceptre was also gilded. There have also been some interesting physiog-nomical changes to the statues since the time H.O. Neil's engraving was carried out.

But there is another mini mystery that sits alongside this larger one. If one believes the myth that the statues are of Brennus and Belinus the founders of Bristol and that these characters date from nearly 500 years before the Christian era, and as part of the recent restoration they have each been provided with a refurbished orb complete with its surmounting cross, and if, for sake of argument when facing them, Brennus is on the left (the one with the new right forearm), while Belinus on the right has a newly gilded sceptre, how were two pagan kings converted to Christianity (in other words, why are they holding

Brennus or Belinus? Pagan or Christian? The right-hand figure at St John's
gateway, Broad Street.

these symbols of Christian faith) nearly 500 years before Christ was
born? An alternative explanation for the objects each hold in their left
hand is that as pre-Christian kings the spherical object they each hold
in their left hand was not a Christian orb but rather, an ancient symbol of royal power that dates back to classical times. Olympian royal
power was signified by the ancient symbol of the pomegranate. If this
is the case, then it is possible that an earlier building was replaced by
the Christian church of St John the Baptist, and the symbols of royalty
were also Christianised. Thus a cross would have been added and the
pomegranates would have been made into orbs, possibly during the
time of the Holy Roman Empire. Such additions would accord with
the following instructions from Pope Gregory, sent to Abbot Mellitus
when he came to Britain in AD 601:

> To his most beloved son, the Abbot Mellitus; Gregory, the servant of the
> servants of God. 'When, therefore, Almighty God shall bring you to the

most reverend Bishop Augustine, our brother, tell him what I have, upon mature deliberation on the affair of the English, determined upon, viz., that the temples of the idols in that nation ought not to be destroyed; but let the idols that are in them be destroyed; let holy water be made and sprinkled in the said temples, let altars be erected, and relics placed. For if those temples are well built, it is requisite that they be converted from the worship of devils to the service of the true God; that the nation, seeing that their temples are not destroyed, may remove error from their hearts, and knowing and adoring the true God, may the more familiarly resort to the places to which they have been accustomed.

If it was true that Bristol had been founded by Brennus and Belinus and therefore has been in existence since around 563 BCE, it would give the city a nice sense of gravitas, but sadly so far there is insufficient evidence to support the belief.

**The Left-Handed Giant**
This story starts on a fine Saturday morning on 27 September 1851 at William Patterson's yard opposite the Mardyke in Bristol, where the second largest ship that had ever come off the Bristol stocks was about to be launched. The huge 3,000-ton ship, a side paddle-steamer, was only a man's height less in length than Brunel's magnificent steamship the SS *Great Britain*. It was built for the West India Mail Steamship Company at a cost of £42,000. Unfortunately, more than fine weather was needed for a successful launch and it was delayed by a number of problems, which meant that it was necessary to wait for the evening tide in order to float the ship out of the dry dock. Although some saw the delay as an omen, all went well and the ship was named *Demerara*, after the town in British Guiana, amid general rejoicings, and many congratulatory speeches, including those from the head of the Royal Mail Steam Packet Company and the ship's builder, William Patterson.

During the following month or so the ship was fitted out in readiness to be taken by tug to Scotland to Caird's yard at Greenock for the installation of her massive engines. To compensate for the lack of engine weight and to keep her stable during the tow she was loaded with 1,200 tons of ballast. Her journey to Greenock was due to start early on the morning of 10 November, when there was a high tide, in order to give plenty of time for the towing crew to manoeuvre the

Launch of the *Demerera*, 27 September 1851.

huge ship down the bends of the River Avon. However, there were delays in getting through the lock gates, believed to have been caused by the weight of ballast that bottomed the ship on the mud. The tide, the second highest in the world at about thirty feet, had turned, and common sense should have lead them to suspend the tow until the following tide.

Working a big ship down a tidal river is always a test of seamanship; frequent depth soundings should be taken and there is always the added danger of unfavourable weather conditions that mean the wind works against the tide, with the possibility of the ship slewing to broadside. The situation is always much worse if the wind sets to leeward because then the ship will go very quickly with the tide and there will be no control over her steerage. It seems that this is what happened to the *Demerara*, but it was made worse by the haste of the tug pilot who was presumably trying to make up for lost time. Reports state that in spite of entreaties to slow down he 'took the ship at a rare pace'. Unfortunately, the cautionary words went unheeded until, rounding the double bend in the river, the ship swung broadside on and firmly wedged bank to bank. The fast ebbing tide left the ship suspended across the river with bow and stern fast on the mud and gravel, while amidships, with its load of 1,200 tons of ballast, was completely unsupported. Not surprisingly the ship buckled and twisted in the middle, splitting seams in the process. It says much for the skill of Bristol's shipbuilders that despite this cruel damage, twenty-four hours of frantic digging and offloading of ballast saw the *Demerara* afloat again. She was moored alongside the riverbank in readiness to return her to the shipyard the following day to assess the damage. Unbelievably the next tide pulled her anchors and the situation was repeated. Yet again the ship had to be extricated from the mud, whereupon she was taken back to Patterson's yard where she was salvaged, sold, and sold again. The subsequent owners converted her to sail and renamed her *The British Empire*.

Another casualty of the 'mishap' was the original figurehead, which became a 'half pay' figurehead, meaning it stayed on shore. For many years the figurehead, representing an Indian chief, possibly carved by E.H. Baily's father (but more likely to have been carved by the firm of R. & T. Williams which at that time worked out 53 The Mardyke, Hotwells, directly opposite William Patterson's yard), was mounted outside Demerara House adjacent to the Stone Bridge. From that vantage point the chief probably gazed wistfully over the River Frome that flowed into the harbour, from which he never managed to escape to the open sea and back to the land of his fathers. Maybe it was this

Replica of the *Demerara's* figurehead.

homesickness that gave rise to the local legend that at midnight, in the days when the centre of Bristol was quiet and deserted, the figurehead, or the Left-Handed Giant as he became known, got down off his plinth and walked around – perhaps looking for a berth on another ship?

However, when the building was demolished in the early 1930s to make way for Gilbert Scott's new Electricity House it was hoped that a new home would be found for the Giant with the Bristol Savages, the artists' group at the Red Lodge, but sadly the West Country climate had taken its toll, and in the move he just crumbled away. Some time later a 'replica' was made. This new version does not reflect the ship carver's artistry that was apparent in the original masterpiece. The new figure, supposedly that of an Indian chief, is heavily bearded making him look like a cross between a North American Indian chief and a Roman gladiator!

The addition of the beard is rather strange as it is on record that Native Americans regarded Europeans as something of a marvel for their white complexions, their unusual dress and their beards. However, there could be another explanation for the figurehead's appearance. Although the ship was intended for the West Indies and Caribbean run as well as Demerara in Guyana, it seems that in New Guinea – not Guyana – the chiefs did look very similar to our figurehead. They were bearded and wore similar decorative headdresses so perhaps the new chief's appearance was a result of a geographical mistake.

Other examples of strange stylistic interpretations can be seen in the Exchange in Corn Street. In the main market hall, the carvings above each of the entrances, east, west and south, are supposed to represent the creatures and peoples seen in each of the three continents, Asia, Africa and the Americas. Have a look; they contain some equally bizarre interpretations. Asia has a camel consorting with a dinosaur, Africa has a crocodile that looks like a duck-billed platypus with attitude, and in the Americas there were apparently parrots the size of eagles.

Back to our figureheads, the main feature in common between the two is the spear in the figure's left hand, hence his appellation of the Left-Handed Giant. However, unlike his predecessor, it seems unlikely that the new Indian chief would dare to get down off his plinth and wander around the centre at night, even if he is armed with a long spear.

It seems the moral of all of these stories and strange beliefs is, never spoil a good story with facts.

# 12

## BRISTOL UNDERPINS NEW YORK

A road in New York built upon the remains of Bristol houses – surely not! Improbable as it may sound the following true story of heroism and civic ingenuity is the outcome of a number of initiatives and unusual circumstances that could probably only happen in wartime.

Our story starts in Bristol's modern city centre where there is a plaque commemorating the fact that during the Second World War the Liberty ships had to return to New York in ballast. The essential ballast – all that was available – comprised the sad remains of Bristol's bombed houses. So how did this strange event come about?

In the dark days of 1940 bomb rubble and debris littered the streets of Bristol and clearing it to provide access for the emergency services was a priority. Lorries were requisitioned to take the rubble to barges on the New Cut where a mooring point was chosen on Clarence Road opposite the Mayor's Paddock Baths (nowadays the Mayor's Arms public house), selected to be away from the main dock area. However, because of this site, the barges had to withstand the rigours of the Avon tide, and the mooring needed very strong bollards, still visible today. In the early stages of the war, the rubble was just taken from here and dumped in the Bristol Channel, an arrangement that continued until the United States entered the war.

In 1941 the Germans were sinking British merchant ships faster than we could replace them. In April alone Britain lost 800,000 deadweight tons of shipping, which left us with severe shortages of food and supplies. To make up our losses, in the previous September a mission from British Merchant Shipbuilding had gone to America with plans for a ship based upon a design by J.L. Thompson & Sons at Sunderland, which was a modification of an original nineteenth-century tramp ship (called tramp ships because they tramped from port to port collecting and delivering cargo as and when available, although some did have regular runs). The then Ministry of Shipping proposed a new design of ship, to be known as 'Ocean' class, which would be 441 feet long with a beam of 57 feet, rated at 10,000 deadweight tons

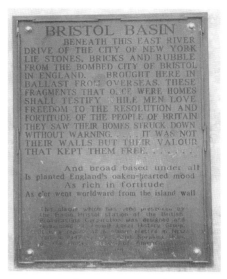

Bristol Basin in New York commemorated in Bristol, England.

with a 2,500 horsepower engine to produce a speed of 10 knots. Although the ship would have been slow, the construction was kept simple in order to maximise production rates. Initially the new ship was classed EC which stood for 'Emergency Cargo'.

Captain Walter Jaffee, Chief Mate on the Liberty ship *Jeremiah O'Brien* during her historic voyage to Normandy for the 50th anniversary of D-Day, and who has written the ship's official biography, explained that the Liberty ships came into being as part of America's innovative response to the situation. The aim was to develop an entirely new production process that would result in ships being built faster than Hitler could sink them, or as President Roosevelt succinctly put it: 'We will build ships by the mile and cut them off by the yard...to build a bridge across the Atlantic'.

The Americans were as good as their word, and for the first time ships that had previously been built on the slips using traditional shipyard practices were designed and built like cars. Shipyards and manufactories across America were swung into action to produce the huge numbers of ships needed to achieve this, requiring nearly twenty new shipyards with a total of 171 slipways. The quarter of a million individual parts required for each ship were made in factories all around the America and then delivered to these shipyards for assembly. The first of these new grey-painted cargo ships, known for their appearance as 'Ugly Ducklings', was the *Patrick Henry*, which took almost five months to build. President Roosevelt said that they would 'Provide Europe with liberty', after which they became known as 'Liberty ships'. After that initial 150-day production cycle, shipyards vied with each other to produce the ships in the shortest possible time – the winners were the Kaiser Shipyards in California who produced a completed Liberty ship in the record time of less than five days.

However, there were problems with the new design. To speed up the production process the ships' components were welded, not riveted, together. For example, the bow section was made separately on the ground and then offered up to the rest of the ship on the slip, where it was welded on. In four war years nearly 3,000 Liberty ships were made, and although 200 were lost, these production rates were instrumental in breaking Hitler's stranglehold on the convoy routes. This was the first large-scale production of ships that were of entirely welded construction, which made them very stiff and unforgiving in heavy seas. Indeed, at one time it was said that British sailors wouldn't sail them unless they had a double row of rivets right around the hull, known as the Insurance Band. The early Liberty ships, especially if without ballast, were prone to split at the seams and even capsize – which is where Bristol comes into the story. It was realised that the bombed remains of Bristol homes being dumped in the Bristol Channel could be better used to provide essential ballast for the Liberty ships bringing much-needed supplies to Britain but returning to the US empty and thus with their stability dangerously compromised. The problem was thus solved when the decision was taken to use the rubble as ballast for the ships when they returned across the Atlantic.

During October 1941 Walter Binger, Borough Commissioner of Works for New York, visited Bristol for discussions on wartime civil engineering projects and was asked: 'What happened to the bomb-site rubble which went to New York as ships' ballast?' His explanation was that most of it was unloaded at the West Side piers where it was taken in barges to the East River to be used as foundation material for the new Franklin Delaney Roosevelt, or FDR Drive, which was later renamed and is now the East River Drive. The highway then under construction on the shore of the East River, near East 25th Street, was the responsibility of Walter who, until that moment, had been unaware that it was specifically Bristol's bombed homes that were the origins of his ship-borne hardcore. Upon his return to New York he made suggestions that a memorial be erected on the shoreline of the drive as close to East 25th Street as possible. He was also moved to approach New York's Commissioner of Parks, Robert Moses, to suggest that the small-boat basin being constructed nearby should be named 'Bristol Basin' as a tribute to Bristolians. The idea was readily agreed and the English Speaking Union of New York was contacted and the proposals explained to James Rowland Angell who, on behalf of the ESU, offered to have a memorial plaque designed and have it installed near the spot. The boat basin was completed in 1942 and on 29 June that year the 'Bristol Basin' was dedicated by Mayor La Guardia, who also unveiled the bronze plaque located on the supporting wall of the footbridge where it crossed the East River Drive at 25th Street.

The Royal Navy was asked to provide a Guard of Honour for the dedication service, and it happened that HMS *Phoebe*, a survivor of the Battle of Greece and Crete, but subsequently torpedoed off Tobruk, was in New York being repaired. The reason for the dedication was explained and the crew was asked for volunteers. To quote a former crewman: 'the Chief Petty Officer was so overcome by the stampede of sailors wanting to volunteer, required an extra tot of rum to prove that he was not dreaming.' The reason was of course that they had just survived some terrible experiences and realised only too well that many of their comrades had not.

The day dawned cold and bright with not only the Royal Navy Guard of Honour in attendance but also the British Consul General in New York and civic dignitaries. Amongst the other guests was the music-hall star Gracie Fields, who, although living in America by that time, always supported the efforts of the British Forces wherever she was through her dedicated work for ENSA (Entertainments National Service Association).

It was also agreed that in Bristol a duplicate of the plaque would be erected at the bridgehead alongside other bronze plaques commemorating key events and achievements in our maritime history. This was put in place in June 1942.

The plaque itself has an interesting history. James Rowland Angell made a perfect choice when he commissioned Stephen Vincent Benét to design the memorial plaque. Benét followed his own wording on the plaque with a very fitting quotation from Bayard Taylor's memorial freedom poem, 'A National Ode'. Benét, a Pulitzer Prize winning poet, novelist, and short-story writer was born in Bethlehem, Pennsylvania and his winning poem, 'John Brown's Body', is still considered the quintessential American war poem.

Angell's choice of Benét for the wording on the original plaques was probably inspired by awareness that he was America's equivalent to our Poet Laureate. 'John Brown's Body', his epic poem of the American Civil War, was only one of his many poems and stories dealing with the apocalyptic effects of war. During the years leading up to the Second World War he had written extensively on the threats posed by the rise of fascism. Because of this and his personal knowledge of Guernica he must have had a heavy heart when asked to provide the wording for these plaques – a poignant reminder that his words of warning during the 1930s had not been heeded. It must have been with mixed feelings that he met Angell's request.

For nearly thirty years the plaque on the supporting wall of the New York footbridge remained, gradually becoming forgotten except for a graffiti writer named 'Joe' whose name was scrawled across it in yellow paint, until in 1970 the Bristol Basin was redeveloped for a waterside apartment complex and the plaque was taken down for safekeeping. At the completion of the building, named the 'Waterside Plaza', the plaque was replaced, in a better site on the riverside wall of the plaza overlooking the Bristol Basin, but still only yards away from the footbridge.

The 1970 rededication of the New York plaque was the occasion for a dramatic ceremony. Bristol's own, the late Archibald Leach better known as the actor Cary Grant, arrived on a red London Routemaster double-decker. The New York ESU also received congratulatory messages from the President of the Bristol ESU, Eric Dehn, his Grace the Duke of Beaufort, Lord Lieutenant of Bristol. The Lord Mayor of Bristol, Councillor Bert Peglar, also took the opportunity to restate the support given to Bristol during the blitz by so many Americans.

By this time Bristol was also in the midst of its own redevelopment with major changes taking place in the vicinity of the bridgehead. The Bristol plaque was similarly taken down for storage and subsequent reinstatement, but was accidentally damaged beyond repair. There the story would have ended but for the persistence of Ivor Davies, whose letters to the civic authorities and local newspapers came to the attention of the

## BRISTOL BASIN

BENEATH THIS EAST RIVER
DRIVE OF THE CITY OF NEW YORK
LIE STONES, BRICKS AND RUBBLE
FROM THE BOMBED CITY OF BRISTOL
IN ENGLAND...BROUGHT HERE IN
BALLAST FROM OVERSEAS. THESE
FRAGMENTS THAT ONCE WERE HOMES
SHALL TESTIFY WHILE MEN LOVE
FREEDOM TO THE RESOLUTION AND
FORTITUDE OF THE PEOPLE OF BRITAIN.
THEY SAW THEIR HOMES STRUCK DOWN
WITHOUT WARNING...IT WAS NOT
THEIR WALLS BUT THEIR VALOUR
THAT KEPT THEM FREE...

"And broad-based under all
is planted England's oaken-hearted mood,
As rich in fortitude
As e'er went worldward from the Island wall."

ERECTED BY THE
ENGLISH SPEAKING UNION OF THE UNITED STATES
**1942**

members of a local history group who decided that it was only fitting that the missing plaque should be replaced.

After many discussions and some diplomatic persuasion, in 1986 a replacement plaque was made, and anyone standing near the bridgehead next to the statue of Neptune, mid-morning on Wednesday, 16 July 1986, would have witnessed the unveiling and heard a dedicatory speech by the Right Honourable Lord Mayor of Bristol, Councillor Joan Jones, who reminded people what the plaque commemorated and that people should not forget all those who lost their lives either in the Second World War bombing or at sea in the ships while attempting to bring us those essential supplies. The replacement plaque, designed and researched by

Temple Local History Group, was donated to the City of Bristol by Derek Woodcock, manager of BBC Radio Bristol. The plaque was made by John Gardiner of Paramount Engraving in Bristol.

However, there is still an unsolved mystery connected with these commemorative plaques. During 1944 the Royal Society of Arts held a competition of schoolwork that included essays and poems from around the country. Fairfield Grammar School in Bristol was involved in a school scrapbook project. Mr R.K. Gilkes, retired Deputy Headmaster of the school remembered that the Fairfield Scrapbook, one of twenty across England, and one of the top four selected, was displayed in an exhibition at the Royal Society of Arts in London early in March 1944. Particular mention was made of the Fairfield Scrapbook on BBC Children's Hour on the opening day of the exhibition. The Head of the English Department of the school in 1944 thought that it was exchanged with one from Danbury High (or Hill) School, near an artificial lake in Lake Candlewood, USA, whose school magazine was called the 'Nutmegge'. It is mysterious that subsequent research has not yielded further information regarding the exact identity or location of the exchange school, although several have been contacted. The Fairfield Grammar School entry selected by the RSA included a poem about the plaque by a pupil, Patricia Jones. Again, for some reason, sadly only the first and last lines of her poignant poem survive. They nevertheless perhaps provide a fitting end to this account:

> The people's churches, homes and shops did fall…
> …and Bristol far away once more
> A pathway laid through western lands.

# 13

# TRIALS AND TRIBULATIONS

**Trial: A Tragedy Behind a Name**
How many people waiting for a bus at the Centre, on Colston Avenue outside the Church of St Mary on the Quay notice the bronze plaque on the pavement wall behind them? Some may glance at it, realise that it is another war memorial and look away. Possibly the only time the

Church of St Mary on the Quay, Colston Avenue.

plaque is given more than a cursory glance is at 11 a.m. on 11 November or on Remembrance Sunday when the crowds are not waiting for a bus, but attending the service at the Cenotaph directly opposite. All across the land, in city, town and village, war memorials exist as a reminder of our loss and of the high price of victory. On each and every memorial, behind the stark list of names, lie stories of family tragedy and heroism. This particular memorial in the centre of Bristol commemorates the members of St Mary's congregation who lost their lives in the First World War. Although it is certain that every name on the plaque has a story associated with it, our interest within the confines of this book is with the very first name on the plaque, that of Archer-Shee, G.

The full name is that of George Archer-Shee whose father, Martin, was the manager of the Bristol branch of the Bank of England in nearby Clare Street. Martin and his family lived above the bank and were all active members of the congregation of St Mary on the Quay and were also involved in local community activities. George served as an altar boy at the church until he left Bristol to attend the great Jesuit College of Stonyhurst in Lancashire. It was planned that George would follow a naval career and so after Stonyhurst he was sent to Naval College from which, it was hoped, he would graduate with a commission in the Royal Navy. Sadly this was never to be. The reason for this was that when George was aged thirteen he became a cause

The first name on the war memorial at Church of St Mary on the Quay.

célèbre through being accused of stealing a five-shilling (25 pence) postal order from a fellow cadet. Although he pleaded his innocence, he was expelled. Many believed in George's innocence, not least because of his moral family upbringing and his Jesuit education. For example, when at Stonyhurst College all the pupils were taught to add the letters A.M.D.G. in the top left-hand corner of every page of submitted work (the letters standing for *Ad Majorem Dei Gloriam*, to serve as a reminder that their every action was 'For the Greater Glory of God'). They were also expected to finish their work with the letters L.D.S. meaning *Laus Deo Semper* translated as 'Praise to God Always'. This was the system of morality that had been instilled in George from an early age, which made the accusation of a mean and petty theft and the resultant blackened name even more shocking.

Although many who knew him and his family believed in his innocence, his father was unable to appeal against the expulsion on constitutional grounds. This was because the Naval Academy was part of the Royal Navy and thus came within the King's domain and as such was above the law. In order to prosecute an action to get a fair hearing to clear his name the family had to obtain the personal permission of the King to pursue the case through the courts. After a lengthy process George Archer-Shee's 'petition of right' was placed before the King, Edward VII, who agreed and signed it, including the phrase 'Let Right be Done'. With the Royal signature and permission, you would have thought that the case could have proceeded, but the Admiralty successfully challenged the petition, getting it overturned. At this point the family, who had a reputation for probity, instructed a foremost barrister of the day, Edward Carson, to raise a legal appeal. This was successful and in July 1910 the case finally went to trial. After only four days the Admiralty dropped their defence and accepted George's innocence. There then followed a period of legal wrangling that involved Members of Parliament and questions being asked in the House. Questioners included George's older brother Martin who by that time was a Tory (Conservative and Unionist) MP. However, in spite of the general support another year was to pass before the Admiralty finally capitulated and paid the family compensation of £3,000 together with £4,120 for their costs.

Although George and his family were vindicated by the outcome of their action he was, unsurprisingly, disenchanted with the idea of a naval career, and after returning to Stonyhurst to complete his education he left this country and went to America to work. He returned home at the outbreak of the First World War and accepted a commission as a Lieutenant in the first battalion of the South Staffordshire regiment. In 1914 he was posted to Ypres but was tragically killed in one of the very first battles, thus ending a sad life that had held so much promise.

Long after George Archer-Shee lost his life he was again in the news. In 1947 a fictionalised account of his case made into a play, *The Winslow Boy*, could be seen at the Bristol Hippodrome. The playwright was Terrence Rattigan, who used the trial events as the subject but changed the characters and relationships. He also set the play in the Second World War, explaining that he wanted the play to be about the 'little man's quest for justice', rather than just about the specific experiences of one family. That said, as a tribute to the family, and with their agreement, the play was premiered in Bristol before opening in London. (More information about this sad but fascinating case can be found in Ewen Montagu's 1974 book, *The Archer-Shee Case*).

**Tribulations**

The three days of the Bristol riots at the end of October 1831 are events that are now firmly set into Bristol's historic calendar. Many books have been written on the subject and by now all the tales have been told…or have they? The following account is an example of how even the 'great and the good' of the city can get caught out by their behaviour – a revelation which of course will come as a complete surprise to many! However, before explaining how this revelation came about, it might help to look back at the circumstances that led to the unmasking of this 'error'.

The riots broke out because of the disaffection of the broad mass of Bristol's populace with the local government, in particular the totally undemocratic organisation of the Common Council and the Aldermanic body. Proposed parliamentary reform of local government, if passed, would have helped to calm the situation but, unfortunately, the proposed Reform Act had been rejected by the House of Lords at the beginning of October, their rejection being due in part to the nearly 200 speeches that the Bristol Recorder, Sir Charles Wetherell, had made against it. The Bishop of Bristol had also cast his vote against it in the House of Lords. As a result of this, local feelings against both the Bishop and the Recorder were running high, especially as 22,000 Bristolians had submitted a petition to Parliament in support of the Act. Local awareness of Sir Charles Wetherell's role in the defeat of the Act, together with his ill-advised visit to Bristol provided both the motive and opportunity for civil unrest, although in light of what followed the term 'civil unrest' turned out to be a wild understatement. The Recorder's visit turned out to be the spark that ignited the powder-keg of resentment.

The riots started as soon as the Recorder's coach from Bath came into view, beginning predictably with name calling, quickly followed by stone and missile throwing, which in the absence of firm control, escalated to threats of further physical violence. The stone throwing soon progressed to the storming of buildings, looting, arson and full-blown anarchy. Detailed explanations of how this came about can be read in any of the books on the subject, such as Peter Macdonald's *Hotheads and Heroes* or Derek Robinson's *A Darker History of Bristol*. One of the main features the Bristol Riots had in common with many others throughout history was the frenzy of looting followed by orgiastic behaviour by the rioters. Sadly, as is often the case, much of what was looted from warehouses, merchants' houses and official buildings was either of no use to the rioters or was damaged beyond repair – with a very singular exception.

The motives and subsequent actions of the rioters were driven by two key factors: avarice and anarchy. The initial targets of the rioters' anger were the houses of the well-to-do merchants who lived in modest splendour in Queen Square. Their houses contained lots of nice shiny things that the rioters coveted. Also, most of the merchants had cellars full of very fine wines, which no doubt included Bristol Milk and certainly, as it turned out, large quantities of the sailors' favourite tipple, rum. Paintings, books, and expensive furnishings were also plundered, most of which fell victim to the anarchistic tendency; ending up being destroyed within the precincts of the square itself or by being carried off to the squalid courtyards and alleys of the city slums. The night of Saturday, 28 October 1831 saw many households that normally ate off stoneware or wooden plates eating off silver salvers with silver cutlery. Others returned home swathed in unaccustomed finery, while some struggled to get totally inappropriate furniture into garrets or closet-sized rooms that were hardly big enough for the occupants let alone a chaise longue or sideboard. However, it was what happened when order was restored that provides us with this interesting footnote to history.

As is often the case with instances of civil disorder, once the decision is made to restore order, no mercy is shown, with civil procrastination switching to draconian retribution. Bristol proved to be no exception as three troops of mounted Dragoons armed with sabres gave no quarter as they chased the panic-stricken rioters through the streets and alleyways of the old city. Although most of the rioters armed with cudgels or paving cobbles were opportunistic, some were obviously intent on more premeditated mayhem.

On the morning after the riots, when the streets were littered with broken bottles, window glass and the remnants of once fine furniture, the Vicar of St Thomas', Reverend Martin Wish, went to open up his church and clear up the mess littering the approaches. On the steps of the church he found a bloodstained cutlass, abandoned in the heat of battle, dropped by victor or victim. He put it in the church strong room for safe-keeping, where it remained for many years awaiting its owner. Was the cutlass dropped by a rioter – perhaps one of those cut down by a sabre-wielding Dragoon? Perhaps the cutlass wasn't dropped by a rioter at all but by an Officer of the Watch, who could have been disciplined for losing it, or even worse the blood could have been his. Once the authorities regained control of the city and the looters realised that retribution was nigh, wholesale panic ensued with them frantically trying to either dump or hide their booty wherever they could. Massive amounts were thrown into the harbour or the river, and even down wells or buried in gardens and graveyards. Sixty years later a rioter's inheritance, a cache of silver spoons, was discovered behind a gravestone in Temple Church yard.

A bloody relic of the Bristol Riots found on the steps of St Thomas' Church.

In spite of what was drunk or destroyed, so much was recovered – forty wagon loads of it – that they had to use the quadrangle of the Exchange in Corn Street to display it, with the overflow being taken to the nearby parish churches. Two wagon loads alone came from a single house in Host Street. However, in the midst of the post-riot panic one person, John Ives, kept a cool, if foolhardy, head.

Amongst the city treasures in the Mansion House was an intricately patterned silver gilt basin or salver and ewer that had been presented to the city by Alderman Kitchen in 1573 (Kitchen, himself a former mayor, also gave the city one of the 'Nails' outside the Exchange). Ives, who had stolen the salver, must have realised that it represented riches beyond his wildest dreams, but he must have also realised that it could also mean a certain trip to the gallows if it was found in his possession. In an attempt to disguise its origins he cut it into 167 pieces before stupidly offering the fragments to a Bristol Goldsmith, Robert Williams. Not surprisingly, local goldsmiths and jewellers had been told to report any unusual offerings and Ives was arrested, with 164 of the pieces being recovered. He, unlike some of his fellow rioters, escaped hanging (probably only because the silver was recovered), but instead was transported to Botany Bay for fourteen years of hard labour. Williams' honesty was rewarded by being given the task of reuniting the 164 pieces, which he achieved by fixing each piece to a new backing plate, and making up the three missing pieces. After the successful restoration it was returned to the Mansion House. A visitor to Bristol, Sir Robert Peel (founder of the modern police force, whose policemen were known as 'Peelers'), was so impressed by the restored salver that he offered to buy it for its weight in gold – his offer was not accepted and the restored salver still has pride of place in the Mansion House display of city treasures. It was said that Williams' goldsmithing skills were such that the beauty of the restored piece was unimpaired and its value enhanced, presumably by the additional weight of the backing plate.

As a bizarre footnote to this incident from the riots, John Ives was one of the lucky ones who survived his fourteen-year sentence to Botany Bay, and upon his return to Bristol asked to see the restored salver. It is unclear whether he was allowed to see it, but it is unlikely, as his request was reported as 'matchless impudence'. I wonder if he said, 'Do I take that as a No?'

But what of the 'great and the good', the victims of the riots? How did they get caught out, and how was their ethical quandary resolved? In order to compensate victims of the riots for damages and losses a Bristol Compensation Act had to be passed. This was necessary because until that time loss commissioners attempting to deal equitably with all those from across the different wards of Bristol would have had conflicts with the existing laws of England as they applied to the ancient divisions of shires and hundreds. This was particularly true of old laws relating to the preservation of the peace and provision of relief to the sufferers of a riot. The new Act allowed for the appointment of commissioners who could deal with all aspects of the damages and the commissioners established a series of hearings to deal with the numerous compensation claims. The 'great and the good' found themselves in something of a quandary, as outlined in the Commissioners' original report:

> The very frequent claims made for losses in respect of silver and jewelry induced the Commissioners to apply to the Corporation of the Poor [the Workhouse] for the aid of some pauper labourers, in order to

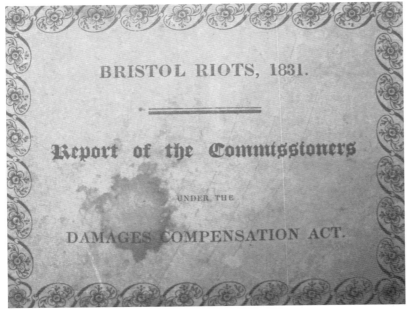

Riot Commissioners' report, 1831.

examine the ruins of destroyed edifices under the supervision of a trust-worthy superintendent. The inferior metals collected in this search nearly repaid the cost incurred in regard to Queen Square, in which however no valuables were discovered.

As a result of their disclosures, several actions for compensation were withdrawn and in the case of some duplicate claims, the plaintiffs were required to elect which claim they wished to be processed. In January 1835 the Commissioners completed their task and in summing up said that '…other data of calculation upon which they can rely afford the Commissioners a perfect confidence in assuming these savings to be at the least thirty-five thousand pounds'. In closing they thanked their Clerk, Mesach Brittan, who received £2,000 for his services. The report lists page after page of claims, including many from households in Queen Square, who had submitted claims for losses of furniture, etc. These negotiated a reduction in claims from nearly £10,500 to just over £4,000, out of the total saving of more than £35,000.

According to Clifton goldsmith Stephen Grey-Harris, at the time of the riots the salver stolen by John Ives, even though it was a fine example of Tudor silver gilt, would probably only have been valued at a few hundred pounds. Compare this with the £6,000 error in the claims that were renegotiated by the great and the good. Then compare what happened to them – nothing – with the sentence of fourteen years' hard labour and transportation meted out to John Ives.

| IM. | SUMS CLAIMED | | | | | | | | | | | | RESOLUTION of COMMISSIONERS | | SUMS RECOVERE[D] | | |
|---|---|---|---|---|---|---|---|---|---|---|---|---|---|---|---|---|---|
| | By Information before Magistrates. | | | By Declaration. | | | By Particulars in Court. | | | By Particulars to Commissioners. | | | For Judgment by Default. | For Final Judgment. | By Verdict. | By Agreement with Com[missioners]. | |
| | £ | s. | d. | £ | s. | d. | £ | s. | d. | £ | s. | d. | | | £ s. d. | £ | s |
| et.............. | .... | ... | .. | 2000 | 0 | 0 | 593 | 1 | 6 | 593 | 1 | 6 | 6th August, 1832 | 3rd Jan., 1833 | .......... | 380 | 1 |
| -Street ......... | 156 | 0 | 0 | 200 | 0 | 0 | 200 | 0 | 0 | 180 | 12 | 8 | 30th July, 1832 | 9th Oct., 1832 | .......... | 98 | |
| -Square......... | 400 | 0 | 0 | 500 | 0 | 0 | 439 | 16 | 7 | 391 | 11 | 3 | 31st July, 1832 | 20th Nov., 1832 | .......... | 246 | 1 |
| , King-Street..... | 138 | 0 | 0 | 200 | 0 | 0 | 160 | 0 | 0 | 126 | 5 | 9 | 4th August, 1832 | 9th Oct., 1832 | .......... | 95 | |
| .............. | 500 | 0 | 0 | 800 | 0 | 0 | 800 | 0 | 0 | .... | .. | .. | | 17th Sept., 1832 | .......... | 470 | |
| and Furniture, &c. | 2500 | 0 | 0 | 4500 | 0 | 0 | 4500 | 0 | 0 | 4648 | 16 | 0 | 30th July, 1832 | 4th Dec., 1832 | .......... | 2937 | |
| Queen-Square.... | 400 | 0 | 0 | 500 | 0 | 0 | 448 | 6 | 0 | 437 | 18 | 6 | 6th August, 1832 | 29th Oct., 1832 | .......... | 260 | |
| -Square ......... | 750 | 0 | 0 | 1600 | 0 | 0 | 1600 | 0 | 0 | 1302 | 12 | 11 | 2nd August, 1832 | 26th June, 1833 | .......... | 309 | |
| quare.......... | 1000 | 0 | 0 | 1000 | 0 | 0 | .... | .. | .. | 1100 | 6 | 4 | 2nd August, 1832 | 26th Nov., 1832 | .......... | 712 | |
| .............. | 117 | 0 | 0 | 200 | 0 | 0 | 200 | 0 | 0 | 166 | 11 | 6 | | 10th Dec., 1832 | .......... | 117 | |
| Square ......... | .... | ... | .. | 2000 | 0 | 0 | 501 | 11 | 6 | 501 | 11 | 6 | 6th August, 1832 | 18th Dec., 1832 | .......... | 336 | |
| .............. | .... | .. | .. | 500 | 0 | 0 | | | | | | | | | | 101 | |

Commissioners' decisions.

# 14

## CONUNDRUMS IN STONE

Most of us, if asked to give an example of humour in stone, would probably refer to a quirky statue or funny face on a gargoyle or a window keystone. In Bristol, as well as some fine examples of these, we also have specific jokes and puzzles incised in stone. For example, who but someone with a sense of humour would dream up a notice that reads: 'Half this wall is the property of…' or hang the letter 'O' on a drinking tankard as a challenge for bibliophiles (see below for an explanation of this in-joke)? Not all the signs are meant to be humorous as some, such as those made by tramps or Gypsies, provide important information for those 'in the know'. Others, such as carved grimacing heads on the keystones above window heads, represent a memory of the old warding myths in which the Celts kept the heads of slain enemies in their houses to act as good luck charms to protect the (new) owner and their house. Similarly, the Gauls also kept their enemies' heads, but nailed them at the front of the house (less smelly), both as a good luck charms and as an undoubtedly deterrent to other potential enemies. Throughout human history the disembodied head has been seen as a powerful talisman, but in more peaceable times this practice became stylised to a stone carving of a head or face above the window or doorway. Houses in Guinea Street, Redcliffe and at the corner of Hotwells Road and Hope Chapel Hill have some fine examples, but apart from carved faces and jokes there are hundreds of stones around Bristol that have inscriptions or carved symbols on them. Some inscriptions are secret messages; others are shorthand (a rebus) in stone; another one, although hidden from view, is possibly a reminder of a long-forgotten dispute; while at least one has proved to be of worldwide historic significance.

**How to Become a Property Owner**
Have you ever had the desire to own a wall but haven't had enough cash to buy a complete one? Well, here in Bristol, someone had exactly the same problem which they resolved in a very simple way. They

bought half the wall and left Bristol Council to buy the other half. The faded inscription testifying to this bizarre situation is still there on a wall on the Centre, alongside the passageway to Old Square Chambers by Orchard Court.

**Levity In Stone**

How many of the thousands of people who use the pathway from Anchor Road to College Green, leading beneath the Norman Gateway, notice the intriguing set of puzzles in stone. When Bristol's new Central Library was first unveiled from behind the scaffolding it was realised that the architect, Charles Holden, had a sense of humour. High on the outside of the staircase tower he had included a number of canting or punning coats of arms as sculpted stone panels. Each of the three panels contains a humorous allusion to a well-known bookbinding term. The first, comprising a sun rising over a bar, signifies a 'raised band'; traditionally leather-bound books have five horizontal raised bands or ridges across the outside spine of the book. The second, shows the forequarters of a calf over an open book, with a knife alongside to represent the term 'half calf', in which the cover boards were only half covered in leather. The third joke shows a quart beer tankard with a letter 'O' hanging from the handle. This represents a common book size, the 'quarto' (larger than the modern size of A5 but smaller and squarer than A4).

When the building was opened on 20 June 1906 a local newspaper, the *Bristol Magpie*, which specialised in lampooning everything and everyone unmercifully, and was usually called 'scurrilous' by its victims, was delighted with Holden's cartoons in stone and its 20 September

Drawing of jokes in stone that can be seen outside the Central Library.

1906 issue proposed their own series of fanciful designs of plaques to brighten up other Bristol establishments such as the Eye Hospital.

## A Bleeding Heart
No, this is not a pejorative term as it is often used nowadays, but is a nice example of medieval humour. Above the centre of the Norman arch of the Abbey gateway, between the Central Library and the Cathedral Close, carved in stone is a bleeding heart impaled by three nails. This represents the rebus of Abbot Newland, known as 'Nailheart'. He adopted this visual pun as his coat of arms. A rebus (nothing to do with the fictional Edinburgh detective of that name) is a device that usually depicts the owner's name in some way. The impaled heart of Abbot Newland's is a very straightforward example. Others used by Bristol's merchants as personal trademarks comprised a unique pattern of lines and geometric shapes incorporating their initials. These were used to mark their goods and documents and provide an interesting link to Bristol's maritime past. Ships could be carrying goods for a number of merchants, and with a largely illiterate workforce it was important that each merchant's goods were easily distinguishable. An example of one of the marks used by one of Bristol's most famous medieval merchants, William Canynge, can be seen on the front of his tomb in the south transept of St Mary Redcliffe Church. (A more recent style of mark that even looks similar are the cattle branding marks that signify the cattle as the property of a particular ranch or farm.)

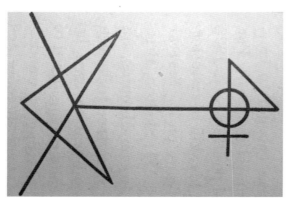

One of William Canynges' merchant marks.

## The Silent Witness

Twenty feet beneath St Nicholas Street on the back wall of a cellar is a stone that is inscribed, 'This is the Boundary of the property of Mr John Wadham, witness F.C. Husenbeath, 1808'. This puzzling inscription raises more questions than it answers. Frederick Charles Husenbeath, born at Mainz in Germany in 1765, was a much respected member of the business community in Bristol where he had lived since 1787. In 1795 he was trading as Husenbeath and Co., Pork Sellers, in St Nicholas Street, and by 1806 the business had expanded and he was in partnership with his son. About that time they opened a further business as wine and spirit merchants, beneath the new market in Baldwin Street, beside the steps leading to St Nicholas Street from Baldwin Street. It could be that the stone marked a boundary between his property and that of John Wadham, and was a polite way of saying, 'this far and no further'.

Another option may be that, as suggested by accounts on the good nature and many acts of philanthropy performed by Frederick Husenbeath, together with his standing in the community, he was the obvious choice as a witness to possibly a long-forgotten property dispute. All that is known about John Wadham is that he could have been the glazier who in the late-eighteenth century had a glass warehouse in Horse Street. Unfortunately this enigmatic stone remains the only, but alas silent, witness.

## Scatological Non-Humour

Not a stone this one but a rusting iron plate on a very old rubble stone wall in the medieval part of Bristol, bearing the inscription, 'Killingworth Hedges Patent Earth'.

No one seems to know what this meant, and local records shed little light. It is just possible that the rusty plate might date from the eighteenth century, at a time when local sanitation was often rudimentary or non-existent; it looked as if it could be related to some form of sanitary innovation. Although today we assume that most toilets are flushed using water, there was a time when the toilet in a shed at the end of garden had advanced from a rudimentary hole in a plank to a number of inventions utilising, if not flowing water, then ashes or other earth-like materials to cover the human waste. Night soil was a euphemism for the byproduct that was collected in carts and taken to the fields outside the city. Thus this plaque appeared to be advertising one of these patent products, perhaps a product based on furnace ashes (a bit like cat litter). However, this was not the case. A search through the patent records for the wording 'Killingworth Hedges Patent Earth – Manufacturers' revealed the manufacturers of this mysterious product were W.J. Furse & Co. Ltd, of Nottingham. The answer to the earthy conundrum had more to do with insurance than toilets.

In June 1752 Benjamin Franklin and Thomas-François Dalibard independently in America and France carried out the now-famous experiments that demonstrated the effects of lightning. Following their experiments, they went on to propose schemes for the protection of buildings from lightning strikes. Further work was carried out by Michael Faraday, James Clerk Maxwell and many others, including Mr Killingworth Hedges. The outcome of the latter's work was that he proposed and patented a practical scheme for the protection of buildings, and in 1905 the Royal Institute of British Architects and Surveyors tasked a group to establish a 'Lightning Research Committee'.

One of the companies licensed to produce Killingworth Hedges' systems for lightning earthing and protection was W.J. Furse & Co. Ltd of Nottingham, which explains why this name is on the bottom of the plate. So 'Killingworth Hedges Patent Earth', it turns out, was a system of metal plates and rods buried in the ground and connected to a roof-mounted lightning rod by heavy copper straps. These protected the building by conducting any lightning strike currents safely to the ground or earth.

This scientific protection against lightning largely superseded the system decreed by the Emperor Charlemagne (742–814 AD), who ordered that each householder should have houseleek or sengreen (*sempervivum*), growing on the roof as a protection against lightning bolts. Nowadays the tradition of having a clump of houseleeks on ones roof continues but generally as a good luck charm in much the same way as an iron horseshoe is nailed above the doorway. Charlemagne's decree was based on reports of the plant's protective and healing properties dating back to classical times when it was believed that it was a magic herb of Jupiter as well as protecting whatever it grew upon from fire and lightning.

## Sacholim or Flowing?

Just before Christmas in 1986 John Martelette's builders were demol-
ishing his existing workshop at the bottom of Constitution Hill prior to
completely reconstructing the building, when some interesting features
were noted. A cast-iron pump close to the rear wall at the hillside end of
the premises indicated the possibility of a nearby water supply and a few
feet to the left of the pump was a small blocked-up stone-fireplace-sized
opening in the stone wall. It had a rebated freestone surround, flush
with the face of the wall. The opening was approximately two feet in
height relative to the floor level. Members of the Temple Local History
Group, having a historic and archaeological interest in the area, decided
to observe progress on the work and, with the owner's permission, took
a series of photographs recording the progress of the work.

During the rebuilding there was an interruption because structural
problems were encountered on the site, relating to stabilising the nineteenth-century rubble-built retaining wall. The uncertain state of the
wall, combined with the steep hillside, necessitated installing a further
reinforced concrete retaining wall. During this extended building
work the fireplace-sized opening in the wall that was packed solid with
general rubbish, including hundreds of old cycle batteries, was cleared.
According to a retired policeman, who had been stationed at the
former Brandon Hill police station opposite (now Avon Wildlife
Centre), the building had at one time been used as a cycle store. Each
evening before setting off on their nightly rounds, the policemen
would fit new batteries to their cycle lights and dispose the spent ones
in the convenient 'fireplace'. When John Martelette's workmen had
cleared it of all the rubbish and sludge, three old pennant stone steps
were found leading down to a muddy sludge. When this was dug out
water was seen about a metre below the 1987 floor level. A massive
freestone lintel was noticed above a chamber with a tunnel-like opening with walls of random stonework and a roof corbelled by a series of
stone slabs reducing in height through to the back of the opening, for
a total distance of about eight feet.

But it was the inscription noticed on the lintel that made history. The
consensus of worldwide opinion was that the inscription on the lintel
stone read as 'sacholim', which translates as 'flowing'. Scholarly opinion
was that the inscription, coupled with the chamber's dimensions and
the existence of the very important high-level outflow, confirmed its

The inscription at Jacob's Well – 'Sacholim'.

function as a Jewish mikveh and, to date, is the oldest one found in Europe. A mikveh is a ritual purification bath, and the importance of this one is that it predates Edward I's expulsion of the Jews from England in 1290. The design, dimensions and use of springs for mikvehs are very strictly defined and controlled in the Mishnah.

Some Jewish historians have suggested an alternative explanation for the use of the spring and chamber: that is as a 'bet tohorah' or cleansing house used in Jewish burial ceremonies. If that hypothesis is correct, the wording of the complete inscription would be 'living' rather than 'flowing' water, yet the arguments for the chamber being a bet tohorah are partly supported by the recorded existence of a pre-expulsion Jewish cemetery further up Jacob's Wells Road, on the site now occupied by Queen Elizabeth's Hospital Grammar School.

Irrespective of whichever historic function proves to be correct, English Heritage recognised the site's cultural and historic significance and in August 2002 it was included as number 28881 on the listing of National Ancient Monuments.

## No. 40 BP 7ft E. Does Anyone Have a Snorkel?
The Poor Law Act of 1601 required all parishes to provide for needy residents. This meant that parish officers did all they could to keep down the numbers of people claiming relief. Unofficial visitors were thus moved on as quickly as possible so as not to be a burden on the parish and old records note the expenses incurred on evicting 'strangers'. For example, an unmarried pregnant woman would be moved to the edge of the parish as quickly as possible in case she gave birth while visiting the parish, with the result that the newborn could claim 'settlement' and its care and upkeep would then be the responsibility of the parishioners. Because of this it was important to know exactly in which parish people lived.

Being bumped on the boundary stones.

In medieval Bristol, with eleven parishes crammed into the area between Christmas Steps and Bristol Bridge, prominent markers were placed at intervals on buildings and roads or wherever space could be found. Each parish had its unique style of lettering or mark – another example of a rebus. For example, St Nicholas parish used a sequence of letters and numbers, in lead or cast iron of the style 'ST N (followed by a number)'. These marks certainly weren't mysterious or funny, unless of course you thought it funny to bump someone on the parish stones as part of the annual ceremony of the beating of the bounds. This bumping ritual was not a cruel joke. The purpose was literally to impress on the youngsters (the future guardians of parish affairs) the boundaries of their parish.

Before explaining the puzzling inscription 'No. 40 BP 7ft E.' there is another macabre tradition associated with life in the old parish. That is the scheme (more often than not, a scam) known as a 'Tyburn Ticket'. Tyburn was the place of the gallows in London and the Tyburn Tree became a name that was nationally synonymous with executions. At one time parish offices and civic duties were just that. If you were appointed to an office it wasn't voluntary, it was a duty, and non-attendance without just cause, similar to jury duty today, would result in a fine. This was in the days when most businesses were family run and for many taking time off to attend to parish matters was very difficult and hence unpopular. Often people did their best to avoid office and the records abound with the names of people fined for not taking up office – particularly if it involved unpopular time-consuming duties such as Surveyor of Roadworks or Overseer of the Poor. However, there was a legal way of avoiding a duty or period of office, without incurring any penalty – one had to be in the possession of a 'Tyburn Ticket'. These came into being in 1699 when 'Any person convicted of burglary, horse stealing or shop theft to a value of five shillings or more, would be hanged'. Upon conviction, the person who had apprehended the thief was entitled to a reward, which came in the form of a certificate that entitled the holder to be discharged from all manner of parish duties for life within the parish where the offence had been committed. The temptation and opportunity for corruption arose, because the ticket could be transferred, once. Tickets were even advertised for sale in the local papers. It is therefore possible that some poor people were falsely accused and sent to the gallows in order to meet the market for Tyburn Tickets. There may even have been instances where the reluctant office holder approached someone who could arrange a convenient 'apprehension and conviction' in order to be able to buy the desired ticket. The *Bristol Journal* for 4 September 1813 ran an advertisement for two tickets, exempting the holders from parish and ward offices of St Paul's and St James' respectively. This iniquitous system, which ended in 1818, is an example of why it could have been dangerous not to know for certain which parish one lived in.

But what about No. 40 BP 7ft E? The oddity about this particular stone is that it is the eighth stone in sequence for the parish of Bedminster.

Bedminster parish boundary mark, at wharf edge, No. 40 7ft East.

What is unusual is that it now lies at the bottom of the Bathurst Basin opposite the Ostrich Inn, seven feet east of the opposite quay edge. Yet when this medieval marker was originally put in place at a bend in the line of the boundary it was on dry land. The joke is that after the nineteenth-century construction of the Bathurst Basin lock, the mayor and other civic dignitaries would have needed snorkels and wetsuits to fulfill the requirements of the perambulation of the parish bounds!

Interestingly, although the hundreds of other parish boundary markers are still on dry land you will still need a boat to see another of them. St Stephen's parish, the city parish, is contiguous with St Mary's Cardiff. Our city parish boundary runs along the River Avon from Bristol out as far as Steep Holme, before going across to Denny Island and back to Bristol. The parish boundaries of both Bristol and Cardiff meet at Steep Holme, where there is a mutual boundary stone against the cliff face at the back of the beach.

**Conundrum: Grown or Carved?**
Near the top of Blackboy Hill set against the pavement edge wall in front of the 1970s petrol station forecourt is a most unusual slab of contoured limestone. It has the appearance of a giant fossilised fern leaf; its fronds, large and distinct enough to see from the other side of the road, branch alternately from the central stem and are, or at least mimic, plant stems. When the holes were excavated for the modern petrol storage tanks, they had to dynamite out the bedrock and perhaps this mystery stone came from those deep excavations. There has long been a worldwide tradition amongst stonemasons of incorporating any interesting 'found items' such as fossils or odd fragments of sculpture into the wall or building under construction. Some other local examples of this tradition can be seen in Christmas Steps, Horfield Road, Tailor's Court and Hotwells Road. If this was really a large fossil fern, could it have been from late-cretaceous times when the slopes of Blackboy Hill might have been covered in a forest of giant fern-like plants (Cycads), complete with groups of dinosaurs?

But, there is possibly a more prosaic explanation. Before being a petrol station and convenience store, this site was occupied by Allens of Bristol 'Blackboy Garage', and before that, the Redland depot for the Bristol Tramways and Carriage Company. An examination of a 1920s photograph of the street shows that the Bristol Tramways and

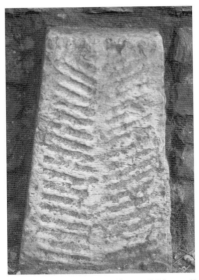

Stone 'fern' next to the petrol station's roadside wall, Blackboy Hill.

Carriage Company frontage was very plain, so perhaps this mystery stone was a carved keystone for a window or door that came from an even earlier house on the site and was found amongst the rubble.

**Pavement Runes**

The word 'rune' is usually connected with something secretive or having a hidden meaning. An entry in *Pears Cyclopedia* listed the code for 'runes' used by tramps or 'Knights of the Road' as they were also known, that was used to let fellow tramps know whether or not a household was worth visiting, whether it provided good food and had generous occupants, or, conversely, whether it contained a fierce dog, so tramps should stay away. However, these 'pavement runes' were not carved by itinerant stonemasons. Have you ever noticed the strange pavement-edge inscriptions that appear on many of the older pennant stone kerbs, especially in the city's older suburbs? These strange markings sometimes also appear low down on garden walls or even by the front doors of houses. It turned out that Bristol's 'pavement runes' represented something completely different and more useful.

The rapid expansion of Bristol into the late-Victorian- and Edwardian-built suburbs coincided with the availability of mains services. For the first time new houses were provided with water, gas, electricity and sewerage – services that we now take for granted. When the residential streets were laid out, the required point of entry from the main road into the house was incised by the service providers on the stone kerb or pavement edge. This showed the house builders where they were expected to dig the trenches beneath the front gardens in readiness for the pipe or cable. Each service provider had their own symbol. At the time these suburbs were built, all the kerb stones were made of hard-wearing pennant stone (a very dense fine-grain sandstone), mainly from the quarries of Messrs Frees at Frenchay who had a long-term contract with Bristol Corporation. These original kerb stones are recognisable by their greenish-grey colour, although sometimes they have a purplish tinge from iron impurities. Each are about 14 inches deep, most of which is hidden, and are hard wearing and fine grained enough to take an inscription.

Another widespread use of pennant stone can be seen in any churchyard in the area where its properties made it ideal for carved gravestones. Examination of the pavement runes and cross checking with householders has shown that an arrowhead symbol pointing towards the house is for gas, an X in a square, for electricity and a rounded capital letter A for water. The symbol for the entry of a water main can sometimes also be seen on the garden wall by the gatepost or even in older houses by the front door or boot-scraper niche. As these have been mostly noticed in terraced houses a likely explanation is that the houses were built before there were pavements to mark. Over the years in addition to these service symbols, others have appeared. Some are in the form of a simple cross, in 2007 often painted in a fluorescent red, green or blue, to indicate to the fire and water companies the proximity of a water hydrant. Another common mark is that of a triangle, often with a central dot, for a theodolite reference point used by surveyors.

This is only a small selection of the many mysterious signs and symbols carved into Bristol's kerbs and pavements. However, before using them to find the location of your water main etc., a word of warning. In recent years the municipal programme of pavement refurbishment has resulted in the taking up of kerb stones, which are then often replaced at a different location. This, of course, completely negates the original purpose of the marks.

**Runes Ecclesiastical**

John Taylor who, in his study of Bristol's ecclesiastical history, tells us that John Robinson, DD, was a Bishop of Bristol Cathedral from 1709 to 1714. A Yorkshire man from Cleasby, Bishop Robinson was a man of many talents. For example he was first appointed Envoy Extraordinary to Sweden, but later became English Ambassador to the Swedish Court, a post he held for nearly twenty-five years. In 1710, while he was Bishop of Bristol, an inscription representing his motto was placed beneath the west window of the cathedral. His long association with Sweden (whilst there he wrote an historical account of the country) could explain why his motto in the cathedral, which translates as 'Man is but a heap of mouldering dust', was not in English or Latin as might be expected but in Scandinavian runes. The inscription (whose characters resembled the long branch Younger Futhark medieval runes of Scandinavia) remained beneath the west window until the nave was extended in the nineteenth century, at which time many memorials such as this had to be moved. It is thought that the runic inscription and other items were stored temporarily in the cathedral cloisters before their hoped-for reinstatement in the new nave. However, it appears that Bishop Robinson's runes joined the long list of the city's historic items that over the years have been removed temporarily for safekeeping, never to be seen again. Perhaps Robinson was more prescient than he realised when he chose his motto, 'Man is but a heap of mouldering dust'. Maybe he had the last laugh, vindicated in memory if not in deed.

Bishop Robinson's runic inscription.

# 15

## THE FIVE THOMASES

The Seven Stars pub became famous in the eighteenth and nineteenth centuries as a favourite haunt of Bristol sailors from the slave ships, which is why, when the Reverend Thomas Clarkson visited Bristol as part of his nationwide information-gathering expedition in support of abolition, he chose the Seven Stars pub as an ideal venue. Much has been written about the iniquitous slave trade, from both a global and from our own local perspective, and this is not intended to be a platform to further the debate. However, during background research for this book, and no book that includes aspects of Bristol's eighteenth-century history can avoid touching on the subject of slavery, a curious connection was noticed: the name Thomas has cropped up in several incarnations throughout the history of the trade. This chapter

The Seven Stars public house, Thomas Lane.

looks at the revolutionary, the anti-slave campaigner, the street, the slave ship and the church, all of which share the name Thomas and have links – either directly or indirectly – with Bristol's slave trade.

## American Revolutionary

Thomas Paine, born in 1737, was the Quaker son of a Norfolk farmer who first came to public attention when, as an excise man in Lewes, he submitted a pamphlet to Members of Parliament in support of better conditions for his fellow excise men. His appeal was unsuccessful and he was not surprisingly sacked from his job. He went to America, which turned out to be the start of his career as a writer and a fighter for people's rights. It was his concept of human freedom which, upon his return to London for the publication of the first part of his paper 'The Rights of Man' in 1787, set the stage and provided inspiration for the efforts of campaigners such as William Wilberforce and Thomas Clarkson. Although most of his reactionary writings caused him problems with the authorities of each of the countries of his residence, England, America and France, it is nice to report that he lived to see the abolition of slavery two years before his death.

## Reverend Clarkson Meets a Disaffected Slaver

It was at a meeting in Bristol in the June of 1787 that the Reverend Thomas Clarkson was introduced to a new member of the Society of Friends (the Quakers). The member, who had previously been involved in the slave trade, had finally become sickened by the traffic and had repented and joined the Society. He was one of the many who came forward during Clarkson's trip around Britain to give their personal accounts of the true situation. That June meeting was also attended by well-known Bristolians who had also become disgusted by the actions of the slavers and who were prepared to publicly voice their support for Clarkson and Wilberforce. During his visit to Bristol it was suggested that in order to get first-hand information about the atrocities carried out by the slaver captains, both against the slaves and their crews, he should visit some of the sailors' haunts. The Seven Stars was chosen because the landlord was against the 'hateful employment' and was known to be willing to introduce him to some of the sailors' discussions. It was proposed that Clarkson should, with the landlord's connivance, pass himself off as a sailor, or at least a common workman, by donning rough non-clerical clothing, wearing a cap, and dirtying his face so that he could mingle with the regulars in order to eavesdrop on the conversations and anecdotes of the mariners. The disguise was necessary for his safety – his stature and red hair made him a marked man for the slavers who wanted to put a stop to his activities.

This subterfuge, also aided by Redcliffe merchant and shipbuilder, Sydenham Teast, whose home was in nearby Guinea Street, was successful. The evidence Clarkson gathered, particularly the stories about the atrocities and impressments of unwilling seamen, he was able to pass to his friend Wilberforce and others. It is likely that, having spoken to the crews of over 300 ships in innumerable pubs and pothouses in his travels around the country, he was well versed in the language and customs of matelots and was able to play the part of a sailor at least for long enough to gain their confidence. All things considered, it does seem strange that the same shipbuilder, Sydenham Teast, who helped the Clarkson gather his information in the Seven Stars in support of the abolitionist cause, was also numbered amongst the attendees of a meeting of Bristol slave traders. The meeting, chaired by a former mayor, William Miles, was held in a coffee tavern in the city only two years after Teast helped Clarkson gather evidence against the self-same slavers. This poses the question: which side was he gathering information for, or was his attendance at both meetings merely insurance?

Although initially the main focus of reformers such as William Wilberforce, John Wesley and Bristol's Hannah More was the effect on the Africans who were being purchased to be sold as slaves in the Americas and West Indies, Clarkson's investigations revealed that the slave captains' inhuman treatment of the slaves also extended to the hapless crews of their ships. The chapter about pirates and privateers discusses the recruitment methods used to crew the slave ships. It was a 'chicken and egg' situation. As conditions on the slave ships became ever more horrible, the captains had to resort to increasing levels of skulduggery to recruit crews, and even more violence to keep them from escaping at the first opportunity. This ill treatment, in addition to the changing moral values, must surely have contributed to the end of the trade. The following tale reveals the extremes to which crews were prepared to go to in order to escape the slave ships.

At the beginning of 1769 on one of Bristol's slave ships, *Black Prince*, the crew decided that they had a better chance of survival if they escaped and became pirates. By capturing the ship's captain and most of his officers, whom they set adrift, they were able to take control of the ship and sail off to a new career under the flag of the Jolly Roger. Unfortunately for them, as part of their preparations they decided to hold a kangaroo court martial of the ship's cook who had upset them – because he sided with the captain or because of the quality of his cooking we shall never know. But what we do know is that the mutinous crew found him guilty and sentenced him to be hung from the yardarm. It wasn't the hanging that killed him, it was the rope breaking. He fell into the sea and was drowned, and it is possible that the captain and his officers witnessed this before being set adrift because just over a year later the authorities caught up with the *Black Prince*, flying its 'Flag of Connivance', in Hispaniola. The ringleader, John Shoals, was brought back to England to stand trial at the Admiralty Court in London for the murder of the ship's cook. His plea that they didn't mean to hang him, just frighten him, but the rope broke, was successful and he was acquitted of murder. However, the bad news was that he was then tried for piracy, found guilty and hanged, and sadly for him the rope didn't break. The name of the ship's cook was McCoy – really.

### The Seven Stars

The present-day pub the Seven Stars, once an inn, is in the lane next to St Thomas' Church. The pub name was a popular one amongst sailors and the picture shown on the modern pub sign in Bristol refers to the constellation known as the Plough, familiar to all sailors navigating by the stars. Another constellation of seven stars that sometimes featured on inn signs frequented by mariners was the Pleiades, or Seven Sisters.

The origins of the name of the inn are, as they say, shrouded in the mists of time and the earliest record that the former vicar of St Thomas', Reverend Marwood Paterson, found when researching the parish history in the 1940s, dated it back to the reign of Charles II. He found that a linen draper, Richard Pope, granted the feoffees of the Church a yearly rent of thirty shillings for a tenement called the 'Starrs', which at that time was in possession of Michael Jaine, who was already recorded as a victualler.

None of the experts on pub signs locally or nationally can say how long the pub in Thomas Lane has held that name; as we all know pubs often have their names changed, often due to a new owner, personal whim or fashion. (However, changes can also come about unintentionally – a Seven Stars pub in Prestwich, Lancashire, played host to mystified customers who turned up at opening time to discover that its name had been changed overnight to 'Same Yet'. It appears that the landlord, when asked by the sign writer refurbishing the sign how he wanted it, was told, 'Oh, Same yet', and so it remained!)

The eighteenth-century landlord, Mr Thompson, who helped the Reverend Clarkson, was very supportive of the local sailors, and unlike the infamous John Barry, landlord of the Harp and Crown on the Quay, is reported to have actively helped the sailors who lodged with him by trying to find them berths on non-slaver ships. He went as far as to say that he 'avoided all connection with the slave trade' and declared that the credit of his house 'would be ruined' if he was known to send those who put themselves under his care into it.

The landlord's help in introducing Clarkson to the sailors during his clandestine visit to the Seven Stars was essential in gaining the sailors' confidence. Clarkson is reported as stating that the atrocities reported were almost too numerous to record, although he made note of a singularly nasty account of a 'punishment' that a hapless sailor had been subjected to by a barbaric slave master. The sailor had been held down and molten tar was then poured on his back which was then cut open with tongs. Sydenham Teast, one of those who had arranged for Clarkson to visit the inn, confirmed the witness's story was true. Clarkson also took copious notes of the underhand methods the slaver captains used to entice or even capture men and boys to crew their ships (as recounted in the chapter 'They May be Pirates, But They're Our Pirates'). With all the information he had gathered, both in the Seven Stars and the stews of Marsh Street, together with that from his other visits around the country, Clarkson was able to provide Wilberforce with sufficient evidence to try to force a vote through Parliament for the abolition of slavery. However it was not to be; Wilberforce's bill was defeated and it was another sixteen years before it succeeded.

## The Ship

A breakthrough in public awareness of the situation arose from an incident that took place on the slave ship *Thomas*. On this ship a crew member died as a direct result of ill treatment by the mate. The court

in London acquitted the mate, which was a tactical error by the supporters of the pro-slavery lobby, because the blatant corruption and
outright lying in the case by the defendants and witnesses for the slave
captains was made public. Sailors who were witnesses against the slavers
had been bribed not to testify, while others had been impressed to sea
so that they weren't available to testify. Although the prosecution lost
the case it nevertheless represented an important milestone in that it
publicised a further element of wickedness associated with the trade,
which in turn contributed to a raised awareness of the true nature of
the traffic in human beings. Public opinion finally began to move
against slavery.

**The Church**
The church that faces the Seven Stars has the dedication to St
Thomas á Becket, the Archbishop of Canterbury martyred in 1170
in front of the altar of his own church. He was murdered by the
supporters of Henry II, who took his words of exasperation with his
troublesome Archbishop literally. Reports say that the King was dev-
astated by the news of Becket's death and did penance at his tomb.
The tomb became a place of pilgrimage and was immortalised by
Chaucer as the destination in his epic *Canterbury Tales*. Ecclesiastical
records dating back to the thirteenth century confirm that our
Bristol church was built on land given specifically for the building of
a church in honour of the saint. However, during the Reformation,
and by a royal proclamation in 1538, Thomas was deprived of his
sainthood and was known just as Bishop Becket. This edict was
repealed by Queen Mary and its dedication reverted to St Thomas
the Martyr, the name by which it is still known today. The church is
still consecrated and, although no longer used for regular worship, it
is administered by the Churches Conservation Trust and is regularly
open to visitors. No doubt the church would have been frequented
by many sailors offering up their prayers to the saint before setting off
on their often-perilous voyages.

# 16

## THE PILLAR BOX AND THE GREAT ESCAPE

Traffic and pedestrians crossing a busy city centre junction little realise that they are passing over one of Bristol's ancient bridges. The Stone Bridge is now invisible because it and the course of the river have been covered over, but it still functions as a bridge over the diverted and culverted River Frome. Nearby was another famous Bristol landmark. It was removed because it was redundant, but due to the public outcry at the time of its removal, promises were given that it would be restored and reinstated as a street feature. If you are a Bristolian there is a good chance that you have guessed what it was: yes, the green pillar that looked like a postbox but wasn't one.

The green pillar, opened by a legitimate user.

Many Bristolians may remember the landmark but may not be aware why this rather incongruous-looking green-painted iron 'pillar box' occupied a prominent place in the middle of the pavement on the Rupert Street side of the entrance to the former electricity board offices. (Although the Electricity Department building, one of Sir Gilbert Scott's famous designs, has been the home to an insurance company for some years, and in spite of its window posters and corporate logos, many Bristolians, if asked for directions that involve it, still refer to it as 'the 'leccy offices' – so much for the power of corporate image makers!) When the door of this 'pillar box' was opened it revealed not a basket for letters but a secret staircase leading down beside the buttresses of the Stone Bridge to the hidden River Frome that still flows beneath the Centre.

Descending into the gloom, noxious currents of air and the murmur of lapping water were the first impressions, until at the flick of a switch, electric lighting revealed a steel catwalk running around one side of a huge vaulted cavern, spanned by a stone arch. The ceiling of the vault is in fact underneath the ancient Stone Bridge. Above the sound of water lapping around the bridge supports were the muffled sounds and vibrations of the city traffic.

Just below the arch of the Stone Bridge are lock gates pointing towards St Augustine's Reach that separate the Floating Harbour from the Frome. Except when the river is in flood, the lock is closed automatically by the pressure of water in the harbour. On the opposite side of the lock gates, but much lower, are the sluggish waters of the River Frome. This river flows from the direction of Rupert Street only to gurgle away through another culvert which is protected by an iron grille to prevent floating debris from entering. It is interesting to note that all manner of objects have been found down there: an underground waterways inspector once trod on something that stuck in his boot which, when removed, turned out to be a Tudor dagger – a memento of dark deeds on the river bank of Lewin's Mead? The same inspector recalled another visit when the smell was particularly awful; it turned out to be emanating from a hapless cow that must have fallen into the River Frome somewhere in the Gloucestershire countryside and been swept downriver and into the culvert where it ended up jammed against the grill under the city centre. He recalled that extricating the decomposing corpse was not one of his most career-enhancing moments.

## The Diversion of the Frome

During the thirteenth century the city was practically encircled by the Frome and the Avon, the only land approach being from the east across the castle ditch or moat. At the narrowest point between the two rivers, Bristol was defended by what was then the second largest castle in the kingdom. To picture Bristol's defences at that time, imagine the two rivers curving around the town, looking on a map like the contours of a bottle, with the castle forming a very effective stopper.

Although the River Frome is still an attractive country stream on the outskirts of the city, flowing through Frenchay and Snuff Mills, once it reaches the vicinity of Pennywell Road and dives underground it is difficult to imagine that it was once a pleasant stream skirting the city and castle defences. In those days, as part of their official duties and annual perambulations of the city boundaries, the city fathers included a visit to Earl's Mead. The highlight of their visit was a feast of locally caught perch and eels, about which a nineteenth-century wit commented that 'the result of such piscatorial art today would more probably be a catch of soles and heels', or to bring it up to date, shopping trolleys, but unfortunately that doesn't rhyme!

Many of the street names in the old part of the city serve as reminders of the river's early history. For example, the names Broad and Narrow Weirs mark the location of the weirs that diverted the Frome around the castle walls and formed the millpond, which was used to drive the castle mill situated just outside the walls. To this day, although the mill and

Magpie cartoon of a city councillor's nineteenth-century boat trip.

even the castle are long gone (we have Oliver Cromwell to thank for that), the marks made by the mill wheel can still be seen underground. Behind the wooden doors at the junction of Merchant Street and Broad Weir are traces on the walls of the ancient mill tail that cuts across from here into the main course of the River Frome at Fairfax Street. The millpond was also connected to the castle's moat that flowed from Broad Weir to the Avon (now the Floating Harbour), just across from the Counterslip. This name is a corruption of the name Countess' Slip, a landing-place once owned by the Duchess of Salop, and now spanned by St Phillip's Bridge, or vernacularly the 'Halfpenny Bridge', a local name which harks back to the days when tolls were charged. Here, at the entrance to the moat, stood one of the city's water gates, and today this entrance can still be seen from Tower Hill as well as from the top of the Riverside Walk on Castle Green.

## The Great Escape from the Pillar

The subjects of the following anecdote will, hopefully, remain anonymous to protect the (slightly) guilty. One Sunday morning a group of eight intrepid explorers decided to carry out an unauthorised exploration of the depths. The door in the green pillar was opened (the handle on the inside used to be an old Morris car door handle) and one of the team stood guard whilst the other seven disappeared as quickly as possible into the depths. The guard stationed above ground had to lean casually against the green pillar, whilst holding the door slightly open, and listen for when his compatriots were ready to emerge.

Panic ensued when a garrulous elderly passer-by decided to stop and explain at length to the guard all about the purpose of the green pillar, opening his remarks with, 'I don't expect you know that it is really an entrance to the river…'. At this point the situation was further complicated by a frantic knocking from inside the pillar, which coincided with the approach of a patrolling Bobby from the direction of Small Street. The guard thanked the old gent profusely, and waved goodbye to him, and then just as the policeman momentarily looked back up Small Street, managed to get everyone out and slam the door shut. However, the old gent looked back and again waved goodbye to the guard, only to see that where a moment before there had been one person now there were suddenly eight orange suited people! He looked a bit bemused and went off shaking his head.

# 17

## ODD TRADES

Over the years many trades and specialist professions have come and gone but however bizarre some of these seem to us now, they were nevertheless once an essential part of everyday life. In the same way, no doubt descendants in a hundred years' time will be bemused by some of today's trades such as 'panel beater' or wonder at such artefacts as a CD ROM. Directories, such as *Matthews' Bristol and Clifton Directory*, include a bewildering variety of trades, many of which are no longer required, and some of which are totally incomprehensible to the modern reader. For example, Bristol had a 'grutt maker'; sadly all attempts to discover the finer points of 'grutt making' have thus far proved unsuccessful. Suffice to say that J.S. Corbett, writing about Dutch and English merchant shipping in the seventeenth century, said that 'the only fare for Dutch fishermen was bread, fish and grutt'. In the absence of any further information we will have to pass on that one for now, but what follows here is a small selection of other Bristol trades and occupations that have disappeared into the mists of time.

During the nineteenth century people were just as fascinated to learn about industrial processes and new inventions as we are today with electronic gadgets. Educational books such as *Common Things* and *How it Works*, together with weekly magazines, *Sunday at Home*, and *The Cottager and Artisan*, all went into great detail about how things worked. In addition to these, a certain class of journalist then, as now, went into factories and other workplaces where they interviewed the proprietors and workforce, and made a living by describing to the public what went on behind the factory doors. One such journalist went by the pen name of Lesser Columbus. He toured the country visiting manufactories, and having the results of his interviews published as a promotional book for each of the towns. Although the descriptions were written to a formula using typical Victorian florid prose – all the premises were light and airy, workers always diligent and happy and the products described were the best available – the books (written in the 1890s) contained considerable detail and provide us with a valuable record of many of our Victorian workplaces. The books usually carried advertisements for the various enterprises, which explained the laudatory language.

Equally valuable to anyone curious about work in Victorian Bristol were the series of sketches produced by the *Bristol Times* and *Bristol Mirror* in 1883. The series of twenty-four articles were also collected and printed as a book and provide us with an understanding of what lay behind the Victorian success of industrial Bristol. Surprisingly, it doesn't mention the other face of Victorian industry – the cholera blackspots, or the houses in Temple with earthen floors, or even the overcrowded slums of Hotwells from where the people came to work in the factories. In one picture of the centre of Bristol looking from Perry Road, twenty-two tall factory chimneys could be counted, each billowing out clouds of black smoke.

Yet in spite of this there were enlightened and compassionate employers such as the Quaker, Joseph Storrs Fry, who founded Bristol's chocolate-making industry in Union Street before it moved to Somerdale at Keynsham (now part of the Cadbury conglomerate), as well as the Wills family, who ran their series of tobacco and allied products factories as paternalistic towns within the city. Their staff magazines often included more details of events in staff lives, right down to betrothals and christenings than many parish magazines, and form a valuable family history resource in their own right. But what of Bristol's old trades; were they really odd or is it just that, overtaken by events, they are meaningless to us today?

### Slops for Sale

There were only two slop sellers on Narrow Quay: Mary Price at No. 24 and a competitor, Mary Robinson, only a few doors away at No. 27. Slops were nothing to do with the dregs at the bottom of a teacup; this was the name for sailors' clothes. With all the maritime activity, the pubs, the instrument makers, block makers, ships chandlers, iron founders, victuallers, sail makers and rope makers, why were there only two entries for slop sellers? One can only assume that most of the sort of places that sold clothes for seamen didn't appear in any business registers because they were sold either as an aside to another business or as casual sales.

## Mouser

In the eighteenth century, at the time of Sir Francis Freeling (see the chapter entitled 'A Fateful Decision'), all the mousers in Bristol were dedicated amateurs. It wasn't until the second half of the following century that mousing became a paid profession and the decision is enshrined in Minute No. 88560 in the archives at Freeling House in London. Even then the first three mousers had to go through a six-month probationary period, during which time they were only paid one shilling per week. This miserly – or 'mouserly' – allowance was not even sufficient to cover the cost of their food and was probably intended to act as an incentive, because they were forced to supplement their rations with mice.

Nevertheless, their employer was pleased with their progress and not surprisingly announced at the end of the six months' probation, that the number of mice in the office had been sufficiently reduced. However, it was another five years before they had a pay rise, and then only by 50 per cent. So who was this enlightened employer? It was the Post Office. The use of cats to keep down the numbers of mice who would otherwise nibble through the signal wires, make nests of the messages and eat the money orders, became a tradition that lasted for over a century.

It was at the end of 1919 that an urgent need for more cats at the Bristol Post Office was identified. The main office had been increasingly plagued with rats, but matters came to a head when one of the night-time cleaners was walking down the stairs and a rat jumped down onto her shoulder. The incident report said that this gave her 'a considerable shock' – a masterpiece of official understatement. Not surprisingly this resulted in more cats being taken onto the payroll.

From time to time the presence of cats on the payroll was queried, and in the 1950s questions on the subject were even raised in Parliament. The issue about the cats' pay and allowances had come to the attention of a number of newspapers and as a result of the adverse publicity the Assistant Postmaster General was forced to reply. He agreed that the cats had not received a pay rise since 1918. He explained that this was because of a general pay freeze and also because it had proved difficult to organise or put in place any form of performance-related pay scheme, but in mitigation, he said that the Post Office hadn't received any complaints from their feline employees!

The *Bristol Evening Post* reported that on Monday, 10 July 1989 the staff of Portishead Radio Station, then run by British Telecom, had just taken on a new member of staff to replace 'Sailor' who had retired after fifteen years of loyal service. The new recruit, named 'Sparks', had the same job as the very first cats in the Post Office's employ: to stop the mice from eating the cables. Because the safety of ships at sea depended upon uninterrupted communication with the Portishead shore station, Sparks' work was vital and, accordingly, he was paid the princely sum of £2 for his board and food, with a bonus of free mice. In the newspaper interview the station manager added that Sparks had an additional role, and that was to stop the mice from eating the radio officer's sandwiches. As far as we know Sparks was the last cat on BT's payroll, and therefore when the radio station closed a few years ago, it brought to an end a tradition that started way back in 1868.

Another Bristol establishment that had resident cats was the Bristol Pottery at Fishponds. Because, as Sarah Levitt recounts in her history of the pottery, the large quantity of straw used for packing was irresistible to mice, they acquired the cats to keep the mice out of the straw. But, as the saying goes, there is no such thing as a free lunch, and the cats in turn used the straw as a nest for their kittens.

## Crimps

These were agents who acted as procurers for the navy and did by guile what the press gangs did by force. They worked on commission and used any method possible to lure unsuspecting young lads onto a ship. It didn't matter to them whether the recruit was vertical or horizontal when loaded onto a boat at the quayside to be rowed down to the man of war waiting at her moorings at the Hungroad, down at Shirehampton. The crimps, as mentioned in the chapter entitled 'They May Be Pirates, But They're Our Pirates' often worked hand in glove with the unscrupulous landlords; those of the stews of Marsh Street being the worst of the lot.

One long-lasting but apocryphal tale associated with crimps or recruiting agents was the tradition of the 'King's Shilling'. As normally recounted, the acceptance of the 'King's Shilling' was supposed to be an acknowledgment that one had been officially recruited. The tale was that one of the crimps' tricks would be to surreptitiously drop a shilling into the mark's tankard of beer, and when the poor unsuspecting soul next drank, it signified that they had 'taken the King's Shilling' and were recruited. Even in those days the practice, if true, seems to be of dubious legality. But perhaps if the hapless and generally ignorant youths believed what the crimp told them, it didn't matter whether it had the force of law behind it or not; once they were on a ship the point was purely academic.

Another story associated with the King's Shilling is that landlords introduced pewter tankards with glass bottoms so that the coin in the beer could be seen before the potential recruit drank from it and thus sealed their fate. Although such tankards can be found in antique shops, and provide a nice souvenir for tourists, and some pubs even have them for their regulars, it doesn't make the tale true. Professor Richard Holmes in his BBC history trail article 'The Soldier's Trade in a Changing World' refers to the King's Shilling being given during the recruitment process. But from the viewpoint of the crimp and his commission or bounty, the only thing that mattered was that he could persuade the gullible recruit to enlist.

As we have seen, recruits were loaded onto the boat vertical or horizontal – in other words, sober or insensible. The term crimping also applied in America, but generally referred to the practice that we know of as 'shanghaiing'. There the agent, often the proprietor of a drinking den, collected a bounty from the shipmaster and, as in Bristol, the drugged or drunk unconscious victims would not usually regain their senses until well out to sea. One notorious American crimper's father died one evening. The loving son, so the story goes, stuck a pipe in his father's mouth, loaded his body onto the boat along with the other evening's haul of unconscious victims, collected his bounty and saved himself the expense of a funeral! Although there is no evidence of a case like that in Bristol, the city still witnessed some rather atrocious behaviour – think of the actions of the infamous Mr Barry, landlord of the Harp and Crown for example.

### Pointmakers
When pottery such as tableware is fired in the kiln the various items have to be kept separate, otherwise the glaze will run and fuse the plates or saucers together into a solid mass. To prevent this happening the items are separated by small unglazed rests, stilts or 'points', which is why on the bottom of nineteenth-century plates or saucers, you can sometimes see three small equidistant pits in the glaze that were made by the points of the pottery rests. The styles of these points varied,

A pottery point or rest that still shows the maker's fingerprints even though it is 160 years old.

depending on the size of the item they were designed to support, and ranged from little tetrahedron-shaped points to larger stars, bars with a triangular cross section, or even stackable thimbles that had a laterally protruding blade to support the plate. Whatever the size, and whether they were made by hand or machine, they all had one feature in common: minimum surface contact with either the kiln shelf, or with the pottery being fired. Nowadays, where used, they are all machine made, but in the 1840s they were handmade.

The example shown here came from the Bristol Pottery and was found during an archaeological excavation carried out during May 1980 on what was then Courage's brewery site on the Counterslip. The pottery used thousands of these rests and the smallest of the points were made by simply pressing the white clay between the fingers to form the small tetrahedrons, a task that was usually carried out in spare moments between other jobs. What is fascinating about these little fragments of Bristol's industrial history is that, when excavated and the earth of 140 years removed, the fingerprints of the person who made them can still be clearly seen.

**Clickers**
Until relatively recently, Kingswood in Bristol was a major centre for boot- and shoemaking. When all boots and shoes were made by hand, one of the tasks was to cut out the leather for the uppers using a metal pattern placed under the leather skin and a small very sharp knife. The skill came in being able to cut the leather effectively so that the maximum number

of shoe uppers could be gained out of a single skin. The operation was called clicking because the only sound to be heard was the click, click, click of a myriad knives against the edges of the metal fashion plate. No music to work by or casual conversation would have been allowed.

## Hecklers

Not Bristol's equivalent to Hyde Park Corner, or even irate rate payers attending Council Committee meetings, but rather the women who in rope making were responsible for the process of taking the initially sorted strands of hemp and teasing it out into strands in readiness for the next stage of the process. With Bristol's past dependency upon maritime activities it is likely that there would have been a number of rope-making works in the city. Before the advent of steel cable the best ropes were made from hemp, with Manilla hemp the most esteemed by sailors whose lives depended upon the quality of the product.

The raw material for the rope making arrived, by sea, in the form of a mountain of tangled plant fibres. The fibres were initially sorted to remove the odds and ends, grit and stones, and were then teased apart by hand into rough strands of fibres, ready for the next stage, heckling, which even in the nineteenth century was carried out using a machine. The purpose of heckling was to take the roughly separated fibres and comb and smooth them out into long narrow strips called slivers, and in this way a yard of hemp became sixteen yards of sliver. After this the fibre passed through a number of drawing processes, each refining and lengthening the resultant strands until they were long and even enough to be spun into the rope. When the process was entirely manual, the spinning was carried out in rope houses or ropewalks, such as the Bryant's rope house (mentioned in the chapter entitled 'Where Are The Doves? The Life and Times of the Templars in Bristol') that was along Temple Back.

## Harbinger

Because of Bristol's strategic position, it has been fought over for centuries, and as a result it has often acted as involuntary host to various armies. With any army, finding quarters for the troops and horses was always a problem. Except for outright conquest, if you hoped to 'win the hearts and minds' of the population, as the current saying goes, some recompense for the hospitality is prudent.

A person or agent who went before the 'protecting army' to negotiate

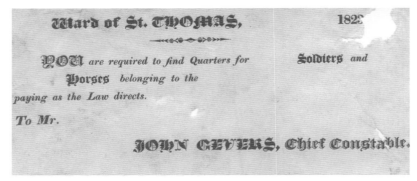

*Ward of St. Thomas,* 182?

*You are required to find Quarters for Soldiers and Horses belonging to the paying as the Law directs.*

*To Mr.*

**JOHN GEVERS, Chief Constable.**

Harbinger's quartering notice for the parish of St Thomas.

for food and quarters was known as a harbinger. Although, as the above notice shows, the word negotiate was applied very loosely – 'you are required to' doesn't sound very much like 'please', especially when the order was signed by the Chief Constable. During the Civil War, with the town being occupied by Royalist and Parliamentary forces on what seemed like a turn and turn about basis, the harbingers must have had a busy time. One wonders how much Cromwell paid to stable his horses in Temple Church?

## Yet More Trades

Lastly, if you want to read about some of the other long-lost trades, Bristol's Central Library has sets of guides and trade directories spanning many years. Remember that in some cases it is only the name that has changed. Consider the trade of 'wardrobe dealers'; nowadays we would consider this to mean a supplier of the item of furniture in which to keep clothes, but as late as the 1960s it meant a person who sold clothes. A well-known example of this particular trade, remembered by many Bristolians, was 'Madame Virtue's Wardrobes' whose business was at No. 6 Lower Park Row. Mrs F.A. Virtue had been at that location for many years, and the University of Bristol students of the flower-power generation searching through her clothes racks for suitably faded finery from their grandmothers' times must have caused her some wry amusement.

The pub next door is the Ship Inn, where students rubbed shoulders with sailors, which takes us full circle back to the two Marys who clothed the sailors by selling them slops from their premises on the Quay.

# 18

## THE DEVIL'S CATHEDRAL:
## RECYCLING EIGHTEENTH-CENTURY STYLE

Next time you pass Ashton Court estate have a close look at the surrounding wall – miles and miles of it – and see if you can spot something curious about it. Nowadays it seems that almost every publication we pick up contains at least one article or chapter about recycling and protection of the environment, and this book is no exception...but with an amazing difference. For Bristolians, recycling is not a new thing – they have been practising it for almost three centuries. Recycling in this instance means the conversion of waste or an unwanted product into a new product, as distinct from re-use. Throughout recorded history, pretty well right up until the 1960s, we had a culture of re-use or 'make do and mend', which during the Second World War became a cornerstone for the country's drive for self-sufficiency. What became a morale-boosting wartime expression arose from a series of Board of Trade leaflets called 'Make Do and Mend' and it was believed that they got the idea from a naval term, 'Make and Mend Day', which referred to the fact that during their off-duty days sailors would use the time to make clothes or other items and to mend equipment.

However, this example of early recycling was also virtue born out of necessity, arising from complaints made about continual obstructions to navigation on the River Avon at Conham, which lies to the east of Bristol. In 1749, the Conham Works of Elton & Wayne were issued with a River Nuisance Report. The Minutes of Common Council, dated 18 August, which can be seen in the Bristol Record Office, contain a record of their complaint which was about 'A great quantity of Cinders laid upon the banks of the said river by the Brass Wire Company, being a very great nuisance and likely to choak up the said river if not removed.' As the company was operating more than thirty furnaces, the amount of 'cinder' was likely to have been prodigious and would have been more than enough to 'choak up the river'. Joan Day who wrote the definitive report about the Bristol brass industry, was of the opinion that the problem of how to get rid of the large quantities of the waste smelting slag (the cinders referred to by the Common Council), probably resulted in Bristol's first and certainly most enduring example of environmental recycling. Nowadays we pride ourselves on increasingly imaginative solutions to recycling problems, but we would be hard pressed to come up with one that surpasses this one. The eighteenth-century Brass and Copper Company came up with a single solution that simultaneously appeased the Common Council, disposed of what by then was probably hundreds of tons of smelting slag from their brass foundry, and at the same time managed to turn the complaint to their financial advantage – in other words make a profit.

Technically the solution was easy: rather than dump the slag into the river when the pot of brass was first skimmed, the still-molten slag was poured into moulds, in the same way that the main product (brass) was. Initially the moulds were simple, producing only rectangular blocks that were about eighteen inches long by about one foot in cross section, and were very black and very heavy. The metal impurities, traces of copper and zinc, gave the blocks an interesting iridescent sheen.

We will never know if it was William Reeve who came up with the brilliant idea of solving the 'nuisance problem'. Reeve was a Bristol merchant, who had married into the Bristol Brass business of the Harford family and would have been in a position to see business opportunities. This was the brainwave: cast the slag into blocks that look like large bricks, that equates to a free building material. Eureka! This is why most eighteenth- and nineteenth-century walls in and around Bristol have at least some of these iridescent black blocks in them. Because of their vitrified structure they make very strong walls. However, their inherent weakness comes from the fact that they are made from solidified slag, and the blow holes and metallic inclusions that give them their sheen means that they are prone to fracturing if placed under too much stress. This is probably why, although they are often seen as insertions in walls, with one very notable exception they haven't been used to build complete walls or buildings.

William Reeves realised that this new building material had to be publicised, but how to do it was the next problem. When his new mansion on the Bath Road was being built, propitiously located on a bend in the road so that everyone could admire his new home and status, he had had the idea of using the black slag blocks to build his stable block and laundry, just across the road from his house, in the form of a black sham castle. He even had a tunnel dug under the road so that staff could get from one part of the estate to the other without having to wait for passing stagecoaches to cross. Or, more likely, the tunnel was used to take his dirty linen from the house to the laundry, obviously heeding the old adage about dirty linen – not in public, and all that.

William realised that if the building was going to advertise the new building material it would have to be spectacularly eye-catching and whatever else he achieved he certainly hit on a winner with this example of self-publicity. Reeves' utterly magnificent stable and laundry block was built in the form of a fake castle, made of courses of the iridescent black slag blocks, alternated with bath stone. On a visit to Bristol, Horace Walpole called it the 'Devil's Cathedral', a name which has stuck. The famous architectural historian, Nikolaus Pevsner, described it as having 'a strange sinister gaiety', while other commentators, Messrs Gomme, Jenner and Little, in their definitive work on Bristol's architectural history, describe Reeves' masterpiece as a 'fantastic toy', and consider it to be the finest early fake castle in Britain.

However one describes it, everyone who sees it agrees that although it may not be in its original sylvan setting, it certainly outshines the industrial drabness that now surrounds it. Apart from the panegyric, did Reeves achieve his probable aim of using his black castle, or the 'Devil's Cathedral' to publicise his new building material? From the evidence and frequency of the black slag blocks in buildings

The Devil's Cathedral: William Reeves' spectacular stables and laundry.

and walls all around Bristol the answer must be a definite 'yes'.

As well as seeing the blocks as additions to many of Bristol's walls, either as coping stones or as actual building blocks, examples have also been found in the region's towns and villages along the Avon, the Severn and the Wye, and as far down as the Hayle estuary in Cornwall, where they have been dumped in the estuary and used as supporting cairns for the channel marker posts. It is likely that these blocks had been used by the coastal traders as ballast – maybe they had the task of clearing the early slag that was 'choaking the river'.

It would be interesting to know if any of these slag blocks made their way to the ports of the New World. The chapter entitled 'Bristol Underpins New York' discusses probably the largest scale and most systematic use of Bristol material as ballast in ships bound for America. Another example of unusual West Country ballast can be seen in Bermuda, where in the town of St Georges, the approach path and steps to St Peter's Church (the oldest in the New World) is paved with a wide miscellany of English bricks, some from the West Country, that were taken there as ships' ballast. William the Conqueror's Bristol Castle was built using Caen stone, as was traditionally a proportion of St James' Priory. Could it be that this stone also came here as ballast?

Apart from the use of the blocks as building material, there was a report that a roadway in St Philips in Bristol was paved with a special design of triangular-shaped slabs of the black slag. However, this has not been confirmed. There is a strong possibility that it was laid as an experiment that didn't work. After all, this would have been at a time before cars, when carts had iron-rimmed wheels and it is likely that the hardness and smoothness of the blocks would have made it almost impossible for a cart to get any traction. But even if that experiment didn't work it seems that William Reeves' self-publicity has given Bristolians a most exuberant example of eighteenth-century recycling.

But what of the wall around Ashton Court estate? Mile after mile of the walls are capped with triangular peaked coping blocks made of the black slag. This would have been a perfect use because they are completely waterproof but, as coping stones, do not need the structural integrity of wall blocks. One wonders what quantity of brass would have been produced to create that number of blocks – a calculation perhaps best left for another day.

# 19

## SERENDIPITY:
## CURIOUS BUT FORTUNATE DISCOVERIES

As well as giving the enduring name to William Reeves' stable and laundry block at Arnos Court, Horace Walpole also coined the expression, 'serendipity'. He first used it in a letter to his friend, Sir Horace Mann, dated 28 January 1754, to describe the '…facility of making lucky and unexpected discoveries'. He went on to explain that he took the name from the three Asian Princes of Serendip who were always making '…discoveries by accident and sagacity of things that they were not in quest of'.

Over the years spent researching Bristol's history this lucky facility has come to my aid and that of my colleagues on a number of occasions. In fact it seemed that our discoveries owed so much to serendipity that a group of us decided to go through our project records and take a closer look to see if they could be classified according to Horace Walpole's definition of the word or whether they were just coincidences or lucky breaks, or whether intuition had made us decide upon a particular path of research. The following list of project researches are just a few examples of research that had surprising outcomes.

### The Start: The Pountney and Allies Plate
A chance visit to the Clifton Antiques Market in the summer of 1979 led to the purchase of a nice but otherwise unremarkable blue-and-white plate to be used as an ornament. The stallholder told me that the Pountney and Allies plate was new stock that had only arrived that morning and because of the popularity of the style he knew it would be sold the same day. It was a chance visit from a friend who, having admired the plate, told me about John Decimus Pountney and Edwin Allies (a short-lived pottery-making partnership), and about the Bristol Pottery that encouraged me to visit the museum to seek further information.

At the time, I was working for a firm new to Bristol, situated on Temple Back just off Victoria Street. At the City Museum a curator told me that the location of our new office block was directly over the site of the Bristol Pottery. When I was shown an old map of the pottery works I realised that the plate had been made 132 years before at the factory area now occupied by my office block and my desk was located on the exact spot where one of the kilns had been.

It was this exciting discovery that got a number of us interested in finding out more about the area where we worked, which subsequently led to the formation of a local history group, which later grew to become Temple Local History Group. Surely this can be classed as serendipity but the next example almost defies description.

## A Mystery Slab of Iron is Reunited with its Offspring

This true anecdote centres on an amazing sequence of events that resulted in a piece of iron found in a Bedminster (or Redcliffe) pub eventually being reunited with its offspring, a clay tile, in Shropshire. The slab of iron featured three inset scenes depicting three monks, one drinking, another smoking, and the third refilling his tankard from a jug.

The story starts in the summer of 1985 following a visit to the Ironbridge Gorge Museum and the nearby Jackfields tile museum at Telford in Shropshire. That visit had been organised by the Bristol Industrial Archaeology Society and included a demonstration of tile making at Jackfields. We had a reciprocal arrangement for information with John Powell, the Librarian of the Ironbridge Gorge Museum, concerning examples of Coalbrookdale ironware that we spotted in Bristol. In exchange John was able to provide us with the provenance and design details of the many items of iron street furniture, such as fountains (including the angel mentioned in the chapter entitled 'Our Missing Angel'), statues, lampposts, etc., dotted around Bristol.

Shortly after the visit, when the demonstration of tile making was still fresh in mind, I saw for sale a slab of iron measuring 6 inches by 12 inches by ½-inch thick, with three scenes embossed into one face of the slab. It looked very similar to the moulds that fitted in a press for making tiles that we had seen on our tour of the museum at Jackfields. The scenes depicted on the slab of iron appeared to be three monks, one drinking from a tankard, the other smoking a clay pipe and the third refilling his tankard from a jug. The stallholder told me that he thought the mould, if that's what it was, had come from a Bedminster (Bristol) pub called the Three Plumes but he was not sure. So far I have been unable to trace any pub of that name in Bedminster, although there was one not far away on Redcliffe Hill. I contacted the museum at Ironbridge who asked me to buy it on their behalf, and we made arrangements that it would be collected on their next visit to Bristol.

For one reason or another eighteen months passed before the mould was collected. When they saw it they confirmed that my guess was correct and that it was an old tile mould. As a reward for the effort they agreed to ask for a tile to be made from it to add to our history group's collection of interesting memorabilia. Nothing more was heard about it but on a subsequent visit to Jackfields in 1987 (by now two years after the initial visit), the mould was seen on display in the museum alongside its offspring tile. Pleased that it proved that my guess had been correct, but upset that they had forgotten their promise, I spoke to the museum staff, explained the background and asked for more details. The following week I received a phonecall with the following unbelievable account.

After my first visit to the museum at Jackfields in 1985 a new curator was appointed who knew nothing of our previous involvement, which explained why the promised tile had never materialised. As a result of the eighteen-month delay in collecting the mould from Bristol, its arrival coincided with the arrival of the new curator, who thought it was just another legacy from his predecessor. It thus remained on his desk as a conveniently heavy item to keep his paper mountain under control. Some time after this the museum had been commissioned to provide a tile from their collection that could be photographed for use as a supporting illustration in a cookery book. It didn't matter what the illustration was as long as it featured a link with food. The department assistant was given the task to search through the museum's tile collection and select a suitable tile. This she did and left the tile on the curator's desk. When the curator came to make arrangements for the photography, noticed that the tile matched his 'paperweight'. He asked the assistant why she had left the mould there as well, to which she replied 'What mould?' They were then checked and found to fit. The museum staff couldn't find out where the mould came from, and a further complication was caused by a gap in their accession book records at that point. However, because it was unusual to be in possession of both the tile and the originating mould, the curator arranged for them to be displayed together. It was only on my second visit two years later in 1987 that the curator learned about the background to the mystery tile mould.

Assuming, as is almost certain, that the tile did come from that mould, did the tile emigrate from Bristol to Jackfields, or did the mould emigrate from Jackfields to Bristol? When did all this take place and who arranged it? Perhaps we will never know.

## Bristol's First Circus and the Fireman

This fireman, Superintendent Gotts, first came to our attention when we were researching an article about the Salvation Army Circus at Stokes Croft in Bristol. Amongst the Salvation Army material loaned to us were details of the disastrous fire at Stokes Croft, together with the name of the man in charge of the singularly unsuccessful fire-fighting team. Shortly after completing the article we received a copy of the Bristol Postcard Club magazine and discovered that it contained a picture of Superintendent Gotts in full-dress uniform and wearing a chest full of medals, but with no other information. Considering that this particular fire-fighting episode had been a disaster, what merited his promotion and inclusion on a postcard? There the story would almost certainly have ended, so imagine my delight when visiting one of our members, to find a book open on his table at the page containing a potted biography of our mystery fireman. It appeared that Superintendent Gotts started work as a Norfolk fisherman, progressed to the London River Police, then became a fireman, and eventually moved to Bristol as Superintendent. The biography included details of his honours and medals, some of which were international acclaims.

The book had been borrowed and was just on that table at the moment in time I happened to be making an unscheduled visit. Does this count as serendipity or was it an example of the result of focussed attention, or even an example of the principle of synchronicity as described by Carl Jung and Arthur Koestler?

## An Apprentice Piece with a Difference

One summer evening, while giving a guided tour of items of interest in the heart of old Bristol, I drew the audience's attention to a splendid street lamp outside the Exchange in Corn Street. One of our elderly members, Jim Yeates, surprised me by announcing that he was glad that I liked the workmanship of the lamp, because it had been his apprentice piece, nearly seventy years before, when he worked for the tin-smiths, T.S

Jim Yeates' proud apprentice piece.

Hall. The ball on the top had been the most difficult part because as a test of his metal-beating skills he had been given a large square of copper sheet and told to form it into a perfect sphere for the top of the lamp!

I don't think that this is true serendipity, probably just a coincidence; however the tale had a nice ending. The account featured in one of our newsletters, which must have found its way to someone in the City Engineer's Office and a couple of years later, when the lamps outside the Exchange were refurbished they arranged for Jim to perform the official opening.

# 20

## SUB ROSA IN TEMPLE STREET AND THE WORLD'S LARGEST NUTCRACKER?

Bristol's strategic importance came to the fore yet again during the Civil War when, at various stages in the conflict, both sides occupied the town. Cromwell's troops are reported to have stabled their horses in Temple Church; that, and the 'great deal of cruelty to many of the principal citizens and Merchants there' shown by Governor Fiennes, were moves guaranteed to have raised support for the Royalist cause. This action might explain why in 1643 the Rose Inn in Temple Street is said to have been the meeting place of Royalist conspirators who, as the saying went, 'met under the rose' because there was a large painted and embossed rose upon its panelled ceiling. The practice of having a rose on the ceiling refers back to classical times when Cupid gave a rose to Harpocrates (the god of silence). A rose on the ceiling thus serves a reminder to guests that discussions within are to be considered confidential, hence the expression 'sub rosa'. For the same reason a carved rose can sometimes be found on the wooden ceilings of confessionals.

The gates out of the city to the south were in Temple and Redcliffe parishes and were only a couple of streets away from the inn. Latimer in his *Annals of Bristol* reported that Redcliffe Gate, with its fifteen cannon, was a scene of fierce fighting during the Royalist siege of the city in 1643. On 26 July 'the enthusiastic Cornish regiments under Lord Hertford accordingly attempted to seize both Redcliffe and Temple Gates but were repulsed with heavy loss'. The Rose Inn later became the Rose and Crown; the name change may have had something to do with the story that Royalist conspirators supposedly met here. Could it be that an overheard conversation in the inn led to the failure of the plot to open the city gates to the besiegers when Prince Rupert arrived with his forces from Oxford on 7 March 1643? The foiling of the plot to open the Frome Gate led to the capture of the ringleaders and to their execution. One of the principals, Robert Yoemans (or Yeamans), a merchant who had served as Sheriff only the year before, was executed outside his own house in Wine Street along with his fellow conspirator, George Boucher. The executions took place in spite of a personal appeal from King Charles for their lives to be spared. Although no one knows for certain how and when the Royalist plotters were betrayed, one theory is that it was loose talk in a tavern that did for them – so much for sub rosa. The moral of that tale must be, if you are a conspirator, there is no point in agreeing to the principles of a sub rosa meeting if you don't make sure that there is no one listening at the keyhole.

The gateway at the bottom of Broad Street, beneath the tower of St John's Church, had a portcullis, and not only can the guide grooves still be seen in the stonework on either side of the arch, but recently the very chains that would have been used to raise the portcullis have been discovered. One can easily imagine the Royalist supporters in the city holding on to these same seventh-century chains while waiting for word that the plot to turn the city over to Prince Rupert's forces had been successful so that they could raise the portcullis. But as we now know, this was not to be.

It is likely that the Reform Act rioters of October 1831 also met here to plan their strategy. Indeed, it was when the coach of Recorder,

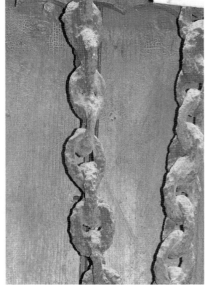

*Left:* Guide slot for the portcullis in the gateway of St John's Church.
*Right:* Surviving chain from the ancient portcullis.

Sir Charles Wetherell, passed through Temple Street that the stone throwing started, and that it was only in the next street that the sword was found on the steps of St Thomas' Church. When the clearing up took place, the section of river that passes through Temple parish provided many wagon-loads of booty. Many years later a cache of silver spoons, identified as part of the loot, was found hidden behind one of the gravestones in Temple churchyard.

Down the centuries, apart from conspirators and Reform Act rioters, many famous people came to the Temple area for a more benign reason: simply to enjoy food and wine. Temple even had its own 'Great Gardens' that the proprietors hoped would rival London's Vauxhall Gardens in splendour. Also high on the list of places to visit was the Stone Kitchen at the Rose and Crown in Temple Street which was famous for its Saturday night tripe and beefsteak dinners.

If nineteenth-century Bristol had a *Good Food* or *Best Trencherman Guide* the Stone Kitchen at the Rose and Crown would probably have featured high on the list alongside other hostelries such as John Weeks' Bush Tavern in Corn Street, the Montague, on the slopes of Kingsdown, and the Assembly Rooms at Hotwells.

On 5 February 1805, those who had been dining at the Rose and Crown were treated to the entertaining spectacle of an elderly oyster stallholder haranguing a member of the aristocracy. This was at a time when oysters were a cheap food for the poor, and not viewed as the gastronomic delicacy that they are today – with, of course, the resultant price tag, which explains why the trenchermen ate inside while the poor stallholder sold her wares to the poor of the parish in the lane outside. Charles Howard was visiting Bristol, and the regular habitués of the Stone Kitchen, knowing his reputation as a trencherman (a person with a prodigious appetite who ate everything put before them, in the days when a trencher was the wooden platter from which food was served), had invited him to one of their Saturday night feasts. His dining companions, likely to have been members of Bristol's Common Council, were probably looking forward to a demonstration of his eating and drinking prowess, as well as listening to examples of his caustic wit.

It is well known that Howard had visited the nearby Temple Church with its famous leaning tower and witnessed its lean before embarking on the evening's drinking. (People coming out of the back door of the King's Head pub after an evening's drinking have looked

Temple Church tower leaning ominously over the King's Head public house.

up at the spectacularly leaning tower and have been known to panic and sign the pledge.) One of the problems with the leaning tower was that whenever the bells were pealed, the tower swayed. A well-known trick that the locals performed in order to impress visitors was to drop small objects down the gap between the tower and nave of the church and watch how they were broken when the bells were pealed. The earliest record of a demonstration of this trick for a visitor was in the sixteenth century, which would have been within a hundred years of the tower's completion. During a visit to Bristol the map trader and geographer Abraham Ortelius was invited to try the experiment with 'a stone the size of an egg', which to his amazement was completely crushed. Ortelius, who flourished during the mid- to late-sixteenth century, is mainly remembered for his cartographic masterpiece, the *Theatrum orbis terrarum*, published in 1570. This is considered to be the first atlas as we would recognise one today.

However, on this nineteenth-century occasion Charles Howard, better known under his title of the eleventh Duke of Norfolk, obliged his hosts by dropping a walnut into the gap between the tower and the nave and watching it explode. As a nutcracker it is certainly very impressive, if a trifle unwieldy. But why was he later harangued by the stallholder? He was coming out of the Stone Kitchen after the evening's meal having, if reports are true, 'eaten like Ajax and drank with twenty Aldermanic power', which could suggest that perhaps he was not too steady on his feet when negotiating the narrow lane (either Bear Lane or Long Row that ran between Temple Street and Temple Back), as he knocked over her oyster stall. She reacted by calling him a 'pot bellied old brute' (it would be interesting to know his response). To refer to his drinking capacity as 'twenty Aldermanic power' would have been praise indeed. The main feature of all the reports of civic ceremonies in Bristol during the days of the Common Council concern the amount of food and drink that was consumed. Perambulations, visits, official openings, were all grist to their desire to stuff themselves with food and drink, presumably at someone else's expense. For example, a perambulation of the city boundary in 1584 started with a breakfast of seven quarts of wine, and two pence worth of cakes and Joseph Leech, reporting on a nineteenth-century visit to the chamber of the Temple Conduit, discussed the lavish refreshments. How things have changed for poor hard-working councillors. It was only in 2006 that there was considerable newspaper coverage when it was reported that free tea and biscuits were provided to lubricate the loquacious in the council meetings. Tea and biscuits: enough to make poor Charles Howard rotate in his grave.

Charles Howard, in spite of strong competition, could certainly be classed as one of the aristocracy's most interesting characters. With his title of Duke of Norfolk he held one of the kingdom's premier earldoms (the family holds the office of Earl Marshal) and he was also a Member of Parliament, a Fellow of the Royal Society, and had also been Lord-Lieutenant of the West Riding of Yorkshire until he was dismissed from the position because of a speech he gave that was considered to be 'politically incorrect'. He was said to have had abhorrence for water – either internally as drink, or externally for washing – but in spite of his prodigious appetite for drink, or because of it, while in Parliament (apart from bursting buttons) he usually appeared clean and refreshed. This was down to a nightly feat of legerdemain on the part of his manservant. Apparently each night when Howard passed out dead drunk his manservant would strip him off, perform the necessary ablutions and change his apparel in readiness for the next day's business, whether gustatory or parliamentary.

The Rose and Crown inn, the local for certain well-known members of the Common Council and other leading citizens, included in its clientele a nationally famous artist, Charles Bird. In his early days as an artist, Bird frequented the Stone Kitchen (in the next street) because it was conveniently close to his 'Evening Drawing School for young gentlemen, near the passing-slip ferry' (now the Halfpenny Bridge). His terms for teaching were one guinea a quarter for three lessons a week, from five to seven o'clock, after which he repaired to the Stone Kitchen. At some stage Charles also repainted the large rose upon the ceiling. This could well have been a fairly regular commission judging by the amount of tobacco that was smoked there. A major collection of Charles Bird's work entitled *Picturesque Old Bristol: A series of fifty-two etchings* was published as a limited-edition two-volume set in December 1885. It was published in conjunction with John Taylor, the City Librarian, who provided him with historic text to accompany his illustrations. His etchings covered all aspects of city life and architecture and represent a nice culmination of his early start giving drawing lessons to young gentlemen on Temple Back. They are also a long way from that early commission repainting the decoration on the ceiling of the Stone Kitchen.

It is nice to be able to provide some continuity between some of the accounts in this twenty-first-century book and the nineteenth-century painting of the rose on the ceiling of the Stone Kitchen. Some of the illustrations in this book have been kindly provided by the family of the artist James Edward (Ted) Bird, who believed that he was possibly a distant relative of Charles. His son Martyn gave us this account of his father:

Edward was born in Bristol in 1893, the son of a successful coal merchant in Cheltenham Road and at an early age showed a talent for drawing and painting. After war service in World War I he returned to civilian life as a commercial artist, and worked for a number of well-known Bristol companies and went freelance in 1950. He had a deep love of his native city, producing a large number of etchings and drawings of Bristol, which he published in book form when he set up in business as J. Edward Bird Press.

James died in 1962 and his sketches and illustrated books are now rare and sought after by collectors.

# 21

## GRUFFY GROUNDS TO LITFIELD PLACE

As strange as it may sound, there is a seemingly unlikely connection between gruffy grounds and Litfield Place; if you don't know what it is, all is about to be revealed. Here is a clue: think 'from plumbago to lumbago'. The answer is lead.

'Gruffy ground' is a mining term, and refers to the rough ground left by open or shallow mining or even quarrying activity. 'Litfield' on the other hand, means lead fields and the place in Clifton of that name refers to one of the sites where lead was mined. According to the Bristol pewterer George Symes Catcott, there was a fissure where lead was mined in what is now Litfield Place (now home to nice residences and medical consultancies). In early mining the technique would have been to work a naturally occurring fissure or to dig simple trenches to follow the vein of galena or lead ore. Hence the clue – plumbago to lumbago – and you could no doubt for the latter receive excellent treatment from the many medical consultants that have set up shop in Litfield House. Apart from being a flowering shrub with nice light blue flowers, plumbago, from the Latin, is also another name for graphite and the source of the name of a person who works with lead, a plumber (although nowadays this has been extended to include other metals and plastic).

However, in the modern city, unless you know what to look out for, there is little evidence of Bristol's historic lead industry. In Bristol, and to the south in the Mendip Hills at Charterhouse and Priddy, lead working has taken place since Roman times and probably all the way back to the Iron Age. The knowledge that lead workings existed hereabouts would have been one of the attractions for the Romans who needed large quantities of lead for their extensive water systems throughout their empire. They used local slaves to extract the lead in the region and indeed, the Roman exploitation of our local resources has been confirmed by isotope analysis, which has shown that even some of the water cisterns at Pompeii were made from our local lead. More tangible evidence came to light when the River Frome, which flows through the centre of Bristol, was being culverted as two lead ingots were recovered from the river at Wade Street. The very heavy 54.6 cm long ingots were stamped: '*Imp[eratoris] Caes[aris] Antonini Aug[usti] Pii P[atris] p[atriae] AD139–161*'; which translates as 'of the Emperor Caesar Antonius Augustus pius father of the fatherland'. (They are now in the Bristol Museum collection.) Considering the Roman loss of these ingots, one wonders what the Roman word was for 'oops', especially as they each weighed nearly ninety pounds. First thoughts after their discovery was that they came from a Bristol lead mine, but the considered archaeological opinion of the day was that they were more likely to have come from the Romans' Mendip mines. This was subsequently confirmed by further studies of the Roman operation of the Mendip mines. One explanation for their internment in a Bristol river bank was that they were en route from the mines to the Roman port of Abonae at Sea Mills.

Long after the Romans had left Britain, Bristol's growing importance led to four monastic orders and other religious houses establishing themselves in or around the medieval town. We will see why the lead was needed if we take the needs of just one of the orders, the Carmelites, as an example. Their order, which was representative of the other monastic houses, required a lot of lead pipe because their system of pipes and tunnels that dates from 1267 was built to carry and safeguard the water from their springs on the upper slopes of Brandon Hill down to their friary on the site of the modern Colston Hall, a third of a mile away. The deep valley of Frogmore Lane necessitated a sealed pipe for that part of the route. In 1376 the Friars generously extended their system to provide water for their neighbouring parishioners of St John the Baptist (the church on the wall at the bottom of Broad Street). After the confiscation of their possessions on 30 July 1538 by Henry VIII during the Reformation, their water supply and pipe, although continuing as a supply for the parishioners, was also put to a number of secular uses.

The growing town needed lead for water pipes, gutters, cisterns, dyeing vats, as well as sheet lead for the roofs of the abbey and the other monastic houses. One reference to the amount of lead used in these buildings was found in a letter dated 30 July 1538 in which the King's Commissioner, making his rounds of the kingdom in order to report how much there was to plunder, wrote to the Secretary Thomas Cromwell:

The Whyte Fryeres [Carmelites] of Bristowe, the whyche all that was in yt ys lytyll more than paid the dettes. Yt is a goody house in byldenge, mete for a great man, no renttes but there gardens. There ys a chapel and an yle off the church and diverse gutteres, spouts and condytes, lede [of lead]…a goodly laver and condyte comynge to yt.

All this goes to show that there was a need for lead, and we know that although there was plenty in the Mendip Hills, Bristolians questioned the need to drag it all the way from there when there were smaller quantities, but probably enough for the town's needs, less than a mile away on Sir Ralph Sadleir's manor of Clifton.

Nowadays the 'Downs' is mainly a smooth open space, but it was not always so. Although it is a flat plateau the edges of Clifton and Durdham Downs were once dotted with quarries, clay pits and lead workings. Most of these have long been filled in to provide Bristolians with a grassy open space suitable for all forms of recreation from football to kite flying (once there was even a racecourse). Names such as Claypit Road, leading off Westbury Road, the gruffy ground, and 'The Glen' are the only reminders of the plateau's former use. The Glen quarry, which many people remember with affection because of the 1950s dance hall that was on the floor of the quarry (out of the sight of parents), has in recent years been replaced by a private hospital that now sits in the quarry like a large brick iceberg with only the upper storeys showing above the quarry rim.

Much of the lead workings on the gruffy grounds have also been filled in, with the rough ground alongside Upper Belgrave Road stretching from the top of Blackboy Hill to Pembroke Road serving as the only visible reminder of the land's previous use. Do the BMX bikers, who see the broken ground with its pits and gullies as a challenge, realise what they are riding over? In the eighteenth century this patch of wild ground was once a place to be feared, as the same rough ground and scrub that provides modern BMX'ers with their cycling terrain also provided highway robbers and ne'er-do-wells with a perfect place to ambush those travelling between Clifton and Westbury-on-Trym. In those days a trip across the Downs was not for the faint-hearted or for those without a well-primed pistol. At a time when justice for those caught was quick and often brutal, a gallows was set up on the road junction at the head of Pembroke Road (then

The gruffy grounds in Upper Belgrave Road.

called Gallows Acre Lane), where the guilty were left to hang as food for the crows and as a salutary warning to other miscreants.

Other evidence for Bristol's local lead industry came from a fourteenth-century reference to a lead-blowing mill. In 1373, Edward III instructed that a perambulation be made of a rivulet called Woodwill's Lake running from Jacob's Well along its course to a conduit of the abbot of St Austins'. The mill, reported to be on the bank of the Sandbrook, now Jacob's Wells Road, would have been on the opposite side of the same hill where the spring for the Carmelites' pipe rose. Owen Ward, who has carried out extensive studies of different forms and types of mills, believes that it is likely that this lead-blowing mill on the river bank would almost certainly have been a smelter that used the water power from the stream running down the valley to drive either bellows or another mechanism to provide a draught for the furnace.

The fact that the local need for lead was met by the local supply (the gruffy grounds workings and the lead fields – Litfields) and processed in at least one documented facility within a mile of the source made good logistic sense and could explain why lead pipes were used extensively in Bristol. Leonard Nott, who had worked in the local plumbing industry for many years and who had also carried out extensive research into the subject, provided the following information on local methods of lead-working techniques which were largely unchanged from Roman times. The lead from the smelter would first have been cast into ingots for storage or transport. The ingots were also known as pigs, because of the way they were fashioned. An oval depression was made in the ground with a number of ingot-shaped depressions coming off one side – looking much like a sow with a row of suckling piglets. The lead was poured in so that it flowed into each of the ingot-shaped depressions, and when it was cooled the ingots could be broken off and stamped ready for transport.

The techniques for manufacturing sheet lead used for cisterns and for pipes were fundamentally unchanged from the medieval period and beyond. Right from Roman times, lead sheets used for covering the roofs of buildings, for making cisterns for water, for dyeing vats and water pipes and for many other purposes, were all produced in a similar manner. Sheet lead was made using a strong table, fifteen to twenty feet long, and five to six feet broad, with an even ledge around it like a billiard table. The top of it was then covered with a smooth layer of fine sand. The ingots, having been remelted in a furnace, were poured into a trough set across the end of the table. The trough full of molten lead was then tilted over to cause it to run evenly over the sand on the table as quickly as possible. Two people, stationed one on either side of the casting table then drew a long board known as a 'strike' over the surface, which by resting on the ledges on either side, enabled them to push forward the superfluous metal leaving a sheet of lead of uniform thickness, equal to the height of the ledge. One firm in Bristol continued to make lead sheet by this method until their premises and equipment was destroyed in a Second World War bombing raid on 24 November 1940. Interestingly the Council House on College Green was the last public building to have a sheet lead roof cast in-situ using this equipment. Smaller sheets, suitable for lead pipe making, such as those for the monastic water conduit pipes, were made in a similar way. The only difference was that a plank of wood, about nine inches wide for the size of pipe in the Park Street tunnels, was pressed into the sand and removed to form a depression of the required size. The lead was then poured into the depression resulting in a piece of cast lead that could then be rolled and soldered to form a pipe.

In those days, plumbing was hard work. The pipes were anything from 11 to 20 feet long and about 4 inches in diameter, each pipe weighing anything from 116 to 177 pounds for an eleven-foot length (based on the distance between the joints in the Park Street pipe), or between 210 to 323 pounds weight for a twenty-foot length. Imagine trying to wrestle a third of a mile of that pipe into a four-foot high tunnel, (the height of the tunnels that run beneath Park Street), and then the pipes still had to be soldered together.

What incentive did the fourteenth-century plumber have for all this hard work? An ancient record book for Bristol, the Great Red Book, has an entry for 1 October 1376 naming a plumber, Hugh White, who was required at his own expense, to maintain the supply of water to the Quay pipe, All Saints' pipe and St John's pipe (the Carmelites' pipe), as well as provide 1,000 feet of strong new pipe per annum. For this service he was to be paid £10 per year, which came from the rents of several houses standing on the bridge at Bristol (in those days Bristol Bridge had houses, shops and a church, much like the old London Bridge). This was for his term of life with the proviso that, if the supply failed for more than six days, he would be fined his whole payment for the year – the full £10. An incentive contract with a swingeing penalty clause! One wonders how some of our modern water supply companies would measure up against that?

The wills book for that century give an idea of the value of the contract to White, and put his salary into a medieval context. They show that the amounts of money bequeathed in estates varied from twenty shillings (one pound) to forty pounds, but that was for a rich burgess of the city. The good news was White had a contract that set him up for life, and he could source his lead locally from the gruffy ground workings or from the Litfields. The bad news was there were a lot of hills that he had to get the pipe up, and the even worse news was that if he didn't deliver he would very quickly starve.

Ancient method of casting lead ingots or 'pigs' from the 'sow'.

# 22

# ECCENTRICS AND UNUSUAL PROPOSALS

Down the centuries Bristol has had a fine collection of eccentrics who have from time to time come up with some curious proposals. This chapter looks at a few eighteenth- and nineteenth-century madcap schemes ranging from flyovers, the tasteful urbanisation of one of Bristol's premier green spaces and Bristol's first shopping mall; well, it would have been if it had been opened as planned but it took them a hundred years to find the scissors!

## Trace Horses

Bristol is, as we all know, a city built on hills. While the hills may be good news for skateboarders, they are not such good news for cyclists and pedestrians, other than those who view them as a fitness challenge – have you tried running up the aptly named Constitution Hill? Back in the days when goods were moved by horse and cart, the hills were a serious problem. When you arrived in the town from the countryside with your wagon of goods pulled by a team of horses, you may not have had sufficient horsepower to even get the wagon into the town over the steep hump of Bristol Bridge, let alone up the hills of Clifton, Kingsdown, Cotham and Knowle; not forgetting of course, the suitably named Totterdown. But if you did manage the hills, you were using more horses than you probably needed for the rest of your journey. Human history has shown that whatever the problem, someone will turn it to their advantage – usually for cash – and the resolution of this particular problem was no exception. The answer was to have stables strategically located at the foot of major hills where additional horses, known as trace horses, could be hired to provide the extra horsepower to get the cart up to the top. One of these stables was on the south side of Bristol Bridge, where the Bristol Foyer hostel is today, being at one time also the site of stables for Georges Bristol Brewery's dray horses. Others were at the foot of Park Street. If you think it is steep now you should have seen it before the viaduct was built at the bottom to bridge the very steep valley of Frogmore Street. For wagon teams making the long climb to Bishopston and Horfield from Stokes Croft, respite came at the foot of Pigsty Hill, where stables, trace horses and refreshment in the form of fodder and drinking troughs could be found at the junction of Gloucester Road and Egerton Road. In addition to the drinking troughs, there was a 20-foot high, green-painted column in the form of a lamp-standard that combined a fountain with sufficient facilities to cater for both man and beast. It even had perches for the birds (actually they were ladder rungs for the lamplighter, but birds have been seen resting there). The fountain was donated as a memorial to Councillor W.D. Watts and is another splendid example of the work of the McFarlane Iron Foundry, and has recently been restored as an architectural feature (rather than a functioning item) by the city. When wagons were superseded by lorries, the road at Pigsty Hill was widened and the horse troughs done away with. By popular request the fountain was kept and relocated to the grassy area of Horfield Common at the corner of Kellaway Avenue and Wellington Hill and remains a handsome reminder of the days of trace horses. There are still a few other reminders around the city in the form of horse troughs. One is on the north side of Colston Avenue, next to the Cenotaph, complete with a dog basin. This one dates from 1908 and was donated:

> In grateful memory of Captain R.B. Nicholetts RN who died August 14th 1908. This trough is erected for the use of animals of whom he was always the unfailing friend and champion. Blessed are the merciful.

Another, St George's Fountain, is at the junction of Summerhill Road and Clouds Hill Road. Apart from providing hired horses as a way of surmounting Bristol's hills, a couple of nineteenth-century entrepreneurs came up with a different solution: don't climb them, circumvent them – not by bulldozing them, but by building flyovers. Unlike the 'temporary' steel one that lasted for twenty-five years to get modern traffic over the choke point at the end of Temple Way, these early flyovers, like Bristol's twentieth-century rapid-transport system, never got beyond the proposal stage.

The first of these systems would have been combined with the urbanisation of almost all of Brandon Hill, including the continuation of Great George and Charlotte Streets right the way around the hill ending near Upper Berkeley Place. Had it been accepted, this proposal submitted in

1821 by Y. and J.P. Sturge to the City Chamberlain, would have made Brandon Hill look like the great ninth-century mosque of Samarra in Iraq. That has a minaret with a great road spiralling around to the summit, which was believed to be have been the inspiration for 1865 Gustav Dorés engraving of the Tower of Confusion (the Tower of Babel in the Book of Genesis). However, here is a curious thought: as the Bristol proposal was dated 1821 and Doré's engraving was produced forty years later, could it possibly be that he heard about the proposal and used it as his visual inspiration? Marc Vyvyan-Jones has produced an interpretation of what the hill might have looked like had the proposal been accepted, which would have reduced this marvellous green space in the heart of the city to a 'tasteful garden' in the top thirty feet of the hill (it was to be another seventy-seven years before Cabot Tower would occupy the summit). As well as the proposal to urbanise the hill, they also proposed 'to ease the declivity from Clifton', by constructing a flyover from Brandon Hill, near the Old Police Station (now the headquarters of

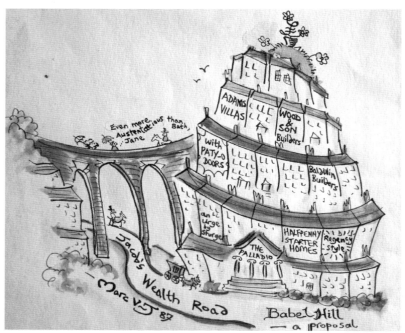

'Babel Hill': an interpretation of Messrs Sturge's tasteful proposals for Brandon Hill.

Avon Wildlife) to the upper part of Constitution Hill, above Bellvue.

A later nineteenth-century scheme, also involving a flyover, was much more ambitious. It was proposed by Joseph King, the builder and amateur architect who was responsible for the design and building of a number of other properties in Bristol, including one that has become a splendid legacy. His flyover was to have soared over the city from Perry Road to Small Street. It wouldn't have been for the faint-hearted but it would have given a nice seagull's-eye view of Christmas Steps, and in passing one could have even leered back at the gargoyles on John Foster's Almshouses. Apparently the Corporation didn't like his scheme – perhaps it would have interfered with their future plans for traffic congestion charges?

Undeterred, Joseph King brought some land in Clifton, just beyond Ferney Close (Victoria Square), in what is now Boyces Avenue, and set about building Bristol's first two-storey shopping mall. He was certainly one for fanciful decoration, as can be seen with the flamboyant property at No. 59 Whiteladies Road, next to the Vittoria pub; this is the remainder of what he hoped would be an arcade of up-market shops to be called the Royal Arcade.

His mall in Boyces Avenue is also a riot of decorative features – oriental outside and fearsome inside. The expression, 'Here there be

Joseph King's thriving arcade.

dragons' springs to mind, especially as the interior is graced with forty-eight of them, complete with supporting gargoyles. Unfortunately, before he was able to open his shopping mall and the adjacent 20,000 square feet of gardens which he styled the 'Royal Bazaar and Winter Gardens' to the public, he went bankrupt. Because it took so long for the mall to open, another theory was that the scissors to cut the opening ribbon were lost, and it took over a hundred years for them to be found. However, whatever the reason, the gardens were sold off to provide the land now covered by the shops of Boyces Avenue and King's Road (sadly the sole public acknowledgement of his vision), and his almost-finished arcade was closed. The arcade was then used for many years as a store for Knee Brothers Furniture Repository, who left the inside completely untouched. In the 1980s I was invited by the owners to a private visit and immediately realised that it was indeed just as Joseph King must have left it in 1878. Everything was swathed in cobwebs, but all the shop units were complete and looked as if they were just waiting for the shopkeepers and stock to arrive. One of the shops even had a moose head complete with antlers looking mournfully down from above, while the serried ranks of dragons supporting the upper floor looked frighteningly fierce. It was a really strange experience, and I almost expected to see Great Expectations' Miss Havisham make a grand entrance from in front of the giant imitation rose window at the far end of the arcade and process down the decorative stairway in all her wedding finery.

The restoration is grand, but with one curious omission: there used to be a motto surrounding the rose window that proudly proclaimed, 'perseverance, progress and success', but a close examination now reveals no trace of the lettering – perhaps now that the site is successful, the reminder is no longer needed. The good news is that once the scissors were finally found the arcade was opened in the early 1990s (sadly not in time to benefit Joseph King) and it has become a bustling hive of activity, which has done much to revitalise this corner of Clifton. His 'Royal Bazaar and Winter Gardens', now called prosaically the Clifton Arcade, is complete with a pub, bookshops, antique shops (and some new ones), a really nice café and restaurant and has become a 'must visit' spot for visitors. No doubt that in spite of the early architectural detractors, the residents of Clifton and the spirit of Joseph King can be justifiably proud of his unique achievement.

# 23

## EDWARD HODGES BAILY RA,
## FROM WAX TO NELSON

This chapter is an account of the amazing sequence of events. To understand what happened and their significance to local history, it may help to begin with a potted biography of this famous Bristolian.

In addition to being a sculptor of national importance, Edward Hodges Baily, born at Downend in Bristol, was both a Royal Academician and Fellow of the Royal Society. Edward was born into an artistic family in Bristol on 10 March 1788. His father, John, was an eminent ship's carver, rumoured to have been responsible for the carving of the original Indian Chief figurehead for the ship *Demerara* that stood for many years outside the Rupert Street side of Demerara House at the end of Colston Avenue. However, in spite of research, so far the family have been unable to confirm this attribution. According to David Brace who started researching the life and achievements of Edward Baily as part of a Temple Local History Group project in 1985, Edward attended Bristol Grammar School, but apparently paid more attention to producing portraits of his school friends than to his studies. Leaving school at age fourteen he was entered into a merchant's accounting office, but office life clashed with his artistic desires and after only two years he decided to leave.

Two of his friends who encouraged his artistic talents were Mr Weeks and a local surgeon, Mr Lee. Until then Edward's main interest had been drawing; however possibly under the influence of Mr Weeks who modelled in wax and who introduced him to that medium, he became interested in modelling. Marguerite Fedden, writing about him, was told that it was the sight of a memorial monument by John Bacon to Mrs Draper in Bristol Cathedral that made Edward decide to turn from drawing to modelling. That said, a major milestone in his life must have been when his friend and patron, Mr Lee the surgeon, showed at least two wax 'models' based upon Homeric heroes of classical antiquity that Edward had completed to his friend John Flaxman, who was so impressed with his work that he invited him to enter his studio in

London. By this time Edward Baily might also have been shown the wax portrait of John Flaxman that had been made by his brother William Flaxman and had been exhibited in the Royal Academy. By then nineteen-year-old Baily had been married for a year but could not afford to turn down the career opportunity to study under Flaxman, so he left his young bride in Bristol and joined Flaxman's studio in London. By the time his wife was able to join him in London a year later his prodigious talent had already been recognised, and although he was only twenty he had already been made an Associate of the Royal Academy, followed by full membership the following year.

He continued as a pupil of Flaxman for seven years before setting up his own at a studio in Percy Street in London. His output as a sculptor was amazing and by 1818 he had already won several medals and monetary prizes, but it was the work he executed for the Bristol Literary Institution, 'Eve at the Fountain', which still has pride of place in the Bristol Art Gallery and Museum in Queens Road that made his reputation.

His first royal patronage came when George IV had him included among the artists to execute the sculpture group in front of Buckingham Palace, as well as the bass relief panels on Marble Arch. Although his major work, 'Eve at the Fountain', is in marble, he also worked in silver, bronze and stone – the latter material being used for what is undoubtedly his most photographed monument. At the height of his career he was justifiably regarded as 'the sculptor to the nation' as this summary of commissions he received testifies: Lord Byron, George Cannings, Sir Astley Cooper, Lord Eldon, Charles James Fox, Earl Grey, Sir Thomas Lawrence, Sir Robert Peel, Lord Mansfield, Lord Nelson, Thomas Telford, the Duke of Susssex (the First Grand Master of the United Grand Lodge) at Freemasons Hall in London, the Duke of Wellington and nearer to home, Southey's monument in Bristol Cathedral and Hannah More's grave tablet at Wrington Church.

However, Edward did not limit his subject matter to political and national figures. He completed many other works, such as the afore-mentioned 'Eve at the Fountain', 'Eve listening to the Voice', 'Girl preparing for a Bath', and the controversial 'Statue of Justice' that surmounts the old Council House in Corn Street in Bristol. When erected, much comment was made because the figure of Justice holds the Sword of Retribution, but has no scales of judgement or balance (an omission that attracted ribald comment from the *Bristol Magpie* newspaper and one that became even more open to debate when later on the building was used to house the Crown Court). Another charming example of his work was 'The Graces Seated'. According to his family the delightful statue of 'Sleeping Nymph' was modelled on his unaware daughter. He found that she had returned home and fallen asleep on a couch, whereupon he took the opportunity to model her impromptu pose.

Following the publication of an article about Baily by the Temple Local History Group it was discovered that one of the group's members, Mrs Frances Charlton, is a relative of his. In her possession was a small, framed, wax silhouette of her great-great aunt Sophia Gould, which had written on the back, 'Wife of John Baily, Mother of Ed. H. Baily, R.A., born in Christchurch, Hants'. It seems likely that this small piece of waxwork was part of the young Edward's youthful enterprise of producing portraits in coloured wax – after all, what would have been more natural for the sixteen-year-old Edward to make this present for his mother using his new found wax modelling skills? If this supposition is correct, the description could have been added when it was either framed or reframed later, when his skill had been acknowledged by the Royal Academy, but before he was made a Fellow of the Royal Society.

*Left*: Wax silhouette of Sophia Gould, wife of John Baily, mother of Edward Hodges. *Right*: Restored portrait of Edward Hodges Baily R.A., FSA, painted by his son William.

Now for the exciting discovery! Frances Charlton also had a large portrait in oils of 'E.H.' that had been damaged during the Second World War blitz of their house in Bristol. It had been rescued, crated up and sent to her brother who lived in Falkirk, Scotland.

In the province of Bristol there is a Lodge of Freemasons named in honour of Edward Hodges Baily, and above the portico of the Freemasons' Hall at the bottom of Park Street is a frieze sculpted by Baily when it was the home of the nineteenth-century Bristol Philosophic and Scientific Institute. Details of his description of the sculpted figures on the panel and their meaning are included, as they show Baily's interest and knowledge of the classical subjects. The frieze represents:

> The Arts, Sciences, and Literature being introduced by Apollo and Minerva to the City of Bristol, who seated on the Avon, receives them under her maternal protection and dispenses to their encouragement and rewards, whilst Plenty unveils herself to peace, since under their happy influence their explanations of the human intellect flourish and improve.

In 1988 following a discussion between the family and the Worshipful Master of Baily Lodge it was agreed that the family would loan the portrait for an exhibition in Bristol. However, it then turned out that the portrait had not been unpacked since that wartime rescue and neither Frances nor her brother knew the extent of the wartime damage. Because of this, and the strong connections with Bristol, the family kindly decided that the portrait should return to Bristol. Accordingly, the crate containing the portrait of Edward Hodges Baily, RA, FRS arrived back in his home city and with great trepidation it was unpacked. The Curator of Fine Art at the City Museum and Art Gallery, Francis Greenacre, had warned that after so many years there might be nothing left but fragments of canvas and mouse droppings, so imagine everyone's relief and delight when the crate was opened to reveal not one picture, but two!

The first was a splendid portrait of E.H. Baily, and the other was a classical study group 'Jupiter and the Dance'. There was more good news when it was discovered that the shrapnel damage was outside the area of the portrait itself and was repairable. The Freemasons very kindly donated the cost of professional restoration that was carried out by the internationally renowned Pelter-Sands Studio, further up Park Street. Thus after nearly 150 years, Edward Hodges Baily, has taken up residence in the hall whose portico he so delightfully enhanced with his sculpted panel. The restorers confirmed that the portrait was painted by Edward's son, William.

There is a rather exciting footnote to this story. Having learned from the article that the statue of Nelson atop the column in Trafalgar Square was sculpted by Baily, and that the Temple Local History Society had no picture of the statue, Nigel Lea-Jones, a professional photographer agreed to obtain one – and used a rather unexpected technique to do so. He wrote:

> The steeplejack firm, Larkins of Essex, have a cleaning contract to regularly remove the 'by products' of the pigeons. Permission was given for me to join the steeplejacks, using their wire and aluminium ladder, to take some photographs of an office block for a client. As the same time, it was possible to take some rather unusual close-up photographs of Mr Baily's handiwork.
>
> The statue stands on a sloping granite plinth, atop the column, and the metal ladder was used to mount the last seventeen feet to his hat, which is approximately five feet from corner to corner. Surprisingly, he is not shown with an eye patch, which is the common depiction of him (his right eye was lost at Corsica in 1794). The only patches are those on his face which, I believe, are stonework repairs necessitated by World War II shrapnel...
>
> Nigel Lea-Jones

Lastly there was another if not curious, but certainly frivolous incident related to Baily's statue of Nelson. Some years ago in an antiques market, an overseas tourist in a group was seen to pick up a small figurine, but noting that an arm was missing, replaced it on the stall. The tourist was about to walk away until persuaded to buy it, the stallholder having assured them that it was in fact a model of the 'infant Nelson'!

# 24

## PREVIOUSLY UNSEEN:
## BRISTOL'S INDUSTRIAL MIRROR UNVEILED

In recent years many books have been written about 'street furniture', which on the face of it sounds pretty boring. However street furniture comprises much more than lampposts, and each item or feature has its own story to tell. Although often overlooked, street furniture clearly reflects a city's industrial past. For example, in the nineteenth century Bristol's rapid urban growth provided extra sideline opportunities for the already well-established engineering industry. Many of the famous industrial engineering firms, in-between building cranes, ships and railway engines were able to use their spare capacity and available resources to make lampposts, drain gratings, coal-hole covers and a multitude of useful things for the growing city. Although the technology and industries have moved on or are no more, their names live on, emblazoned on the city's cast-iron street furniture.

For this reason the names that survive even today, on lampposts, drain gratings, bollards, public clocks and park benches, read like a roll call of the industrial giants of Bristol. The engineering works for which nineteenth-century Bristol was famous – names such as, Peckert, Lysaght, Avonside Engineering, Langford, Parnall, Stothert and Pitt – were already geared up to meet the new market at minimal outlay. It didn't matter if the order was for a loco' furnace door or a manhole cover; both required the same materials and techniques to make, just they needed a different sand mould.

For example, Douglas Motorcycles were famous for their Isle of Man TT winning bikes, but the name can still be found on Bristol's manhole covers and lampposts. Other items of street furniture often have odd stories associated with them. For example, the number eight, has both pro- and anti-Royalist connections. At Hazlebury Road in Knowle and Owen Grove in Henleaze are two of the very few surviving Royal Mail pillar boxes that have the Royal Cipher of the King who wasn't – Edward VIII. While in Lansdown Place and Sion Hill in Clifton, which one might have expected to be staunch Royalist territory,

Royal Mail pillar box at Owen Grove, Henleaze, bearing the Royal Cipher of Edward VIII.

there are two pillar boxes with no cipher at all. Apparently it was eight years before the omission was noted. Or maybe people have long memories and the omission was a local reaction to the use of St Andrew's Church by the Royalist forces under Colonel Henry Washington during the Civil War. So next time you pass one of the older cast-iron lampposts or even a drain grating, have a look – you might be surprised at the name you see. For example, some of the drain gratings in Bishopston still have the name Parnall on them, which was a far cry from their usual products of weighing scales, washing machines or even planes and near St Michael's on the Mount, there is a lamppost marked Bristol Aero Engines.

## Beneath the High Street Obelisk
Is this an example of Egypt in the middle of Bristol? No, but it is a lid on another key aspect of Bristol's development that intrigued Samuel Pepys during his visit. Like the green cast-iron pillar, this obelisk also conceals an entrance to underground Bristol. The Egyptian-looking

This obelisk stands at the High Street entrance to medieval cellars.

entrance that one feels should have a bell marked 'toot and come in' is a novel entrance to one of the surviving ranges of Bristol's medieval cellars. The obelisk entrance is in fact a postwar innovation, erected to safeguard the otherwise bare opening to such a cellar. Before the entire east side of the High Street was destroyed during the bombing of he Second World War, this spot was the location of a famous Bristol restaurant called the 'Posada' and Frederick Jones in his book *The Glory that was Bristol* referred to the restaurant's vaulted cellars that ran from there down to the waterfront. Although they are now blocked off, the former riverside loading entrance can still be seen from Bristol Bridge. It is possible that this also served as a secret entrance to the merchant's cellars from their ships so that they could avoid some of the customs dues. The cellars still have fine ribbed vaulting and other gothic features. They provide a reminder of this novel aspect of Bristol's trading history, and why in Bristol and Madeira sledges were mandatory. Long before London's famous congestion charges, wheeled traffic was banned from the centre of Bristol. In the absence of such traffic, Bristolians had to come up with another form of transport; they copied from Madeira the idea of using sledges to transport the merchants' wares, which became quite a fashion from the Middle Ages through to the seventeenth and eighteenth centuries.

Almost the whole of the medieval town was riddled with cellars such as this one, which were used by merchants to store their precious stocks of wines and Madeiras. The generally accepted story is that sledges were mandatory in the old town because wheeled carts were not allowed in case the rumbling of the iron-rimmed wheels disturbed the wine maturing beneath. Another factor in the banning of wheeled traffic was that in some instances, even now, there is only a pavement-slab thickness separating the road surface from the void beneath. In fact, there was an occasion when a bulldozer being used to clear an old site in the city for redevelopment broke through and fell into the vaulted chambers beneath. Fortunately the driver had been warned beforehand what to expect and was able to jump clear.

However, there are two other explanations for the use of sledges, one of which also has to do with money. John Latimer in his *Annals of Eighteenth Century Bristol* noted an agreement between John Blackwell and the city that allowed him, for a fee (fine), to enjoy the profits arising from the income on 'wheelage' for one whole year commencing 29 September 1743. He was collecting a long-obsolete toll of 3d on every cart bringing goods through the city gates. Therefore a way around the toll, which appeared to be illegal anyway, was to offload the goods at the city gates onto sledges. There is a famous painting in the Bristol City Museum and Art Gallery showing goods on sledges being taken along St Augustine's Parade (just past the end of Denmark Street).

The other equally pragmatic reason for using sledges was that there just wasn't enough room. An article in the *London Magazine* for May 1741 commented on the problem of the narrowness of Bristol's streets. Even in today's modern city, by going along Leonard Lane from the bottom of Corn Street it is possible to get some idea of how narrow the lanes of medieval Bristol really were. This lane follows the line of the old city wall, and part way along on the left is a flight of steps descending through the thickness of the wall to the lower (outside the old city) level of St Stephen's Street. Continue along to the end of the lane where a short dark passage through the buildings brings you to Small Street and Bell Lane opposite. But before you leave the confines of the lane, now empty and almost deserted, imagine the houses overhanging from either side, almost blotting out the sky, and the centre of the lane piled with ordure. Also imagine the lane full of people, dogs, pigs and various other livestock and that you are trying to negotiate a cumbersome iron-wheeled cart through this. When you go through the dark passage at the end of the lane have a close look at the left-hand wall (opposite the signs on the right wall of a bricked-up medieval doorway). The deep grooves in the wall were caused by wagons being tipped sideways by the camber of the lane and gouging their way along the wall.

There are two other features in this part of the lane that are connected with the problems of moving goods around the old town. The first are the stone kerb blocks that are a feature of most old streets in Bristol. These were put in place in an attempt to keep the cart wheels from damaging the buildings. As one can imagine there were many cases of people being maimed and killed by carts or even the wheel hubs crushing people against the walls. If you were caught in a lane such as this there was no way of escaping. The other features in the lane that can be seen throughout the older parts of the city are the nineteenth-century castellated iron kerbs. It would be nice to be able to say they were another local product, but these were made in the Midlands. Their purpose was both to protect the pavements and to provide the cart drivers with something to brake against.

On a lighter note, both figuratively and literally, but still on the subject of iron kerbs, if we go out of the darkness of Leonard Lane and back to the Bristol Bridge end of Welsh Back there is more iron kerb separating the modern pavement slabs from the granite cobbles. Notice that in the middle section of the pavement the half-inch high castellations are worn almost smooth. This is because until about fifteen years ago these marked the entrance to a flight of steps down to public toilets. Even allowing for the fact that in the early twentieth century many workmen passing here would have worn nail studded 'Blakeys', boots, one can't help but wonder how many trips of relief it took to wear down half an inch of cast iron.

Medieval Leonard Lane, showing damage caused by carts tilting against wall.

# 25

## CURIOUSER AND CURIOUSER

'Curiouser and Curiouser' said Alice, which makes one wonder if Mr Dodgson (aka Lewis Carroll) had visited Bristol and if it was the sights and odd things that he saw here that inspired him. This thought came to mind when I remembered the name of the author of a short history of Bristol for children written early in the twentieth century and published in London. The author's name? Dodgson Bowman.

### Anchor With a Difference
With the move of the port from the centre of Bristol, down to the river mouth, a new use had to be found for the docksides. As we all know they have been revitalised or 'gentrified' in order to attract tourists and white-collar businesses that are moving to Bristol for the pleasant environment. Because of this change of use, the docks, which apart from marinas and some specialist boatyards, have been tided up and in the main converted to dockside restaurants and other places of entertainment. Included in this 'tidying up' has been the collection and re-distribution of interesting bits of nautical memorabilia. Although no parrots on perches crying for pieces of eight have been spotted, a banner-carrying pirate has been seen leading a group down Narrow Quay, presumably looking for a suitable plank to walk his party of tourists along.

The British anchor with a Nazi swastika.

Displayed on the quayside is a rather large and curious anchor. The casting proclaims it to have been made in Sunderland, although worked onto one of the flukes in welding bead was a swastika. Although it was just possible this was actually the ancient symbol for good fortune, closer examination revealed this was definitely a Nazi swastika as the arms of the cross point in a clockwise direction. During the Second World War did we supply the German navy with anchors, or was it captured from a British ship, upon which the Nazis made their mark, before we captured it back again? Whatever the answer to this, it goes to show that even seemingly mundane items can have an interesting or puzzling past.

## Broad Gauge Rail

Brunel, who brought the benefits of rail travel to Bristol, along with ships, a hotel and of course his rather famous bridge over the Avon Gorge (which he called 'My first child my first darling'), had one major problem in that there was a difference of opinion over the width his railway. In what became known as the 'battle of the gauges' Brunel's supporters unfortunately lost and so today, instead of his gauge that was just over seven feet wide between the rails, we are stuck with a measly four feet eight inches. This might sound ever so slightly partisan but in terms of stability the broad gauge was superior. Unfortunately, vested interests won the day, and on 20 May 1892 the last of Brunel's broad-gauge trains headed this way from London. In Bristol, fittingly, a small section of this track remains and can be seen alongside its narrow-gauge successor. The view from the edge of Bathurst Basin facing up Guinea Street shows traces of old line that ran into the tunnel under Redcliffe. At this point Brunel's supporters may be forgiven for wiping a tear from their eyes.

## Mystery Tower on the Clifton Downs

At the top of Pembroke Road in Clifton, where once stood the gallows that gave the road its original name of Gallows Acre Lane, is a mystery tower. Very occasionally puffs of smoke have been seen coming out of the top, which prompted someone who knew the history of the site to ask if the gallows had been converted into another instrument of execution. The explanation has to do with transport and is about as prosaic as you can get. The tower is one of a pair; the other is on the far side of the Downs in a valley called Walcombe

Slade that runs down to the River Avon. The towers are ventilator chimneys for the railway line that runs from Clifton Down to Severn Beach. For the short section that runs under the Downs, ventilators are probably not as necessary as they were in the days of steam.

## The King's Pipe

There used to be another chimney in Bristol that smoked, but every time it did, it caused great sadness in certain quarters and grim satisfaction in others. The chimney in question was on the Customs House when it was still in Queen Square. The reason for the sadness and its nickname, 'the King's Pipe', was because the chimney was the outlet of a furnace where any contraband tobacco that had been seized was officially destroyed by incineration.

## Swords into Ploughshares – Metaphorically

Continuing the theme of curious things, dotted along the docksides are seemingly boring bollards – but not if you take a closer look. These bollards, about three or four feet high, and generally on the wharf edge, are used by ships for mooring. They look like cannon stood on end, and that is exactly what some of them are. Particularly after the Napoleonic Wars, there was a surplus of armaments and the age-old tradition that cannon upended in the dockside or river bank make jolly good mooring posts was thus continued here. There is at least one on Welsh Back that close examination reveals to be an upended cannon filled with cement. (This tradition is apparent outside Bristol; indeed, a very old Turkish cannon is used for this purpose on the quayside in Rhodes.)

Other post-Napoleonic mooring posts may look like cannons but aren't. The clue to these posts is the rounded top that is reminiscent of a cannon ball protruding from the muzzle; that is exactly what it represents and reflects the expression 'beating swords into ploughshares'. After the war, when times were hard, naval arsenals looking for new markets hit on the idea of casting cannon using the existing moulds but with a false round to block the open. Thus they made these false cannons specifically to sell to towns for use as street bollards. Their original function may have been forgotten, but the style lives on, which explains why many modern bollards still have the characteristic cannon shape.

## A Yellow Brick Road

Once iron-wheeled carts were allowed inside the old town as distinct from sledges (as mentioned in the chapter 'Previously Unseen: Bristol's Industrial Mirror Unveiled'), apart from some appalling road accidents there was the problem of noise. Iron wheel rims on granite cobbles made things even worse and in the nineteenth century, when castellated iron kerbs were introduced, the noise must have been indescribable. This period was the heyday of the clipper ships sailing to Australia, and they brought back a solution. Long before Australia started exporting wool, the country exported wood from the hardwood tree *Eucalyptus marginata*. Known as Jarrah, this is one of the hardest of the Australian woods and its resistance to insects, water and fire means that it is still prized for these qualities today. In the early twentieth century it was cheap enough to be used as a road surface and was used extensively in London. By the 1930s wood blocks for use as a road surface had also been introduced to Bristol. At that time Bristol had over 417 miles of roads and out of this a total of 11½ miles were paved with these blocks.

The wood blocks made for a much quieter and resilient road which must have also pleased the cart horses. As recently as 1995 Broad Street was still paved with these blocks – they were still visible until the 1970s, but then had to be covered with tarmac because of an unanticipated problem with motor traffic. However, where the tarmac covering had broken away opposite John Street, the wooden blocks were still visible. Although they were good news for horse-drawn traffic, the oil and rubber from motor cars made the surface like a skating rink, which is why they were either removed or covered over.

At one time the stretch of Cheltenham Road at the junction with Gloucester Road was paved with these Jarrah blocks with spectacular results. During extensive floods in the early part of the twentieth century, the whole of that stretch of road was under water for a considerable amount of time. The wet wood eventually swelled and, with nowhere to expand to, in the middle of the road the wood surface rose slowly and majestically out of the flood waters looking as if a large whale was surfacing. The 'bubble', as reported, was about three feet high and the problem signalled the end of Bristol's very own yellow brick road.

**Donkey Walk**
No this is not some bizarre West Country dance routine, neither is it a beach promenade at Weston-super-Mare. It refers to the route the carriers took when unloading goods from beneath the Addercliff. The place and the path known locally as the Donkey Walk have seen many and varied comings and goings over the centuries. The first person to take shelter in the nearby caves was reputed to be King Alfred, and the name Alfred can still be seen inscribed in the stonework over the wharf edge, though be warned, it can only be seen either from a boat or by a contortionist!

In the sixteenth century the site was a mustering place for troops who were about to set off to fight against Philip of Spain. In the eighteenth century a grand parade of houses was built along the top of the cliff and a wealthy Guinea merchant who lived in one of the new houses also bought the wharf and renamed it King's Wharf. During this time Mr Watts, who had his innovatory tower above his house on Redcliffe Hill, dug down beneath his house into the caves in order to get a greater drop for the lead and thus make finer shot.

Donkey Walk and an entrance to the caves at Redcliffe.

More recently, when the Midland Railways had a depot here and used the caves for storage, its name was changed once again, this time to the Midland Wharf. During the Second World War the caves were used as an air-raid shelter, and nowadays they are a sporadic tourist attraction. To sum up, over the centuries countless feet have trudged up the ramp which is the Donkey Walk leading from the dockside to the top of Redcliffe Parade: soldiers, sailors, sea captains, merchants, captives and tourists have all passed this way.